DAVID TORRANCE is a freelance writer, journalist and broadcaster who specialises in the politics and history of the long-running debate about Scottish independence. After being educated in Edinburgh, Aberdeen and Cardiff he worked as a newspaper and television reporter before taking a brief career break to dabble in politics at Westminster. For the past nine years he has been a freelance commentator as well as the author or editor of more than a dozen books about Scottish and UK politics, biography and history. Like all good Scotsmen he has lived in London for long stretches, and is currently based there. A keen traveller, he has visited every Member State of the European Union and more than 120 countries around the world.

Luath Press is an independently owned and managed book publishing company based in Scotland and is not aligned to any political party or grouping.

By the same author

The Scottish Secretaries (Birlinn, 2006)

George Younger: A Life Well Lived (Birlinn, 2008)

'We in Scotland': Thatcherism in a Cold Climate (Birlinn, 2009)

Noel Skelton and the Property-Owning Democracy (Biteback, 2010)

Inside Edinburgh: Discovering the Classic Interiors of Edinburgh (Birlinn, 2010) (with Steve Richmond)

Salmond: Against the Odds (Birlinn, 2010, 2011 and 2015)

Great Scottish Speeches I (ed.) (Luath Press, 2011)

David Steel: Rising Hope to Elder Statesman (Biteback, 2012)

Whatever Happened to Tory Scotland? (ed.) (Edinburgh University Press, 2012)

The Battle for Britain: Scotland and the Independence Referendum (Biteback, 2013)

Great Scottish Speeches II (ed.) (Luath Press, 2013)

Britain Rebooted: Why Federalism Would be Good for the Nations and Regions of the UK (Luath Press, 2014 and 2015)

Scotland's Referendum: A Guide for Voters (Luath Press, 2014) (with Jamie Maxwell)

100 Days of Hope and Fear: How Scotland's Referendum was Lost and Won (Luath Press, 2014)

Nicola Sturgeon: A Political Life (Birlinn, 2015)

General Election 2015: A Guide for Voters in Scotland (Luath Press, 2015)

EU REFERENDUM 2016

A Guide for Voters

DAVID TORRANCE
IN ASSOCIATION WITH THE ELECTORAL REFORM SOCIETY

Luath Press Limited
EDINBURGH
www.luath.co.uk

First published 2016

ISBN: 978-1-910745-51-9

The paper used in this book is recyclable.
It is made from low chlorine pulps
produced in a low energy, low emissions
manner from renewable forests.

Printed and bound by
Bell & Bain Ltd., Glasgow

Designed by Tom Bee

Typeset in 10.5 point Din
by 3btype.com

Contents

Acknowledgements

I would like to thank my brother, Michael Torrance, whose superior knowledge of the workings of the European Union and its institutions were invaluable in saving me from both factual errors and omissions. John Edward from Scotland Stronger in Europe (part of Britain Stronger in Europe) also checked the typescript for accuracy and balance, as did researchers from Vote Leave. Neither campaigning organisation, however, officially endorses this publication and any remaining mistakes are, of course, my own responsibility.

LEAVE

VERSUS

REMAIN

ARGUMENTS FOR AND AGAINST EU MEMBERSHIP ACCORDING TO CAMPAIGNERS

LEAVE	REMAIN
45% OF British exports go to the EU. As a member, the UK avoids exporter tariffs and red tape, as well as obtaining better trade terms due to the EU's size.	The UK will negotiate a new relationship with the EU without being bound by its laws, and will be able to secure its own trade deals with countries such as China, India and America.
For the £340 per year per household which the UK pays to the EU, the yearly benefit of membership is approximately £3,000. This payment is required to access the single market.	The UK sends the EU £350 million per year, which is equivalent to half of England's school budget. This money could be put to much better use within the UK.
EU regulation reduces red tape and benefits business by creating one European standard. By staying in, the UK can push for better regulation.	Leaving would give control over areas such as employment law and health and safety back to the UK, which would be good for business.
Leaving won't reduce immigration. Countries which trade with the EU from outside have higher rates of immigration than the UK has currently.	The UK will be able to change the "expensive and out of control" system which offers free entry from the EU and keeps out non-EU immigrants who could contribute to the UK.
Staying in means that the UK will continue to be represented twice at international summits, by both the foreign secretary and the EU high representative.	The UK has relatively little influence within the EU. If it left, it could take its own seats on international institutions and ultimately be a stronger force for free trade and co-operation.

Introduction

Darren Hughes

As the UK's longest-standing democracy organisation, the Electoral Reform Society has been standing up for voters' rights since 1884. And this is no less the case than with the upcoming EU referendum.

We've been asking how well informed the public feel about the pros and cons of Britain's membership of the EU. The results are worrying – polling commissioned by the ERS suggests that only 16 per cent of voters feel well informed about the issues.

That means that everyone involved in the referendum should be doing all they can to boost public knowledge and engagement in this crucial vote. We saw in Scotland during the 2014 independence referendum what can happen when people feel informed about an important decision and are empowered to take part – record voter registration, citizen-led debates and a huge 85 per cent turnout.

People are crying out for the full information they need to get to grips with the EU referendum debate, and for the space to have those discussions. We know that there is a clear link between how well informed people feel and their likelihood to vote. So we need to foster a deep and vibrant debate around the real issues – not the personalities.

That's why this book is a timely intervention. David Torrance brings his usual strong assets to this book – incisive and clear writing combined with the balanced and unbiased journalism we have come to expect from his work. His previous books have generated diverse debate and informed discussion. David's recent book on the issues pertaining to the 2015 General Election was an immensely helpful guide to voters in deciding who to support. His ability to distill what is important among the haze of claim and counter-claim serves the reader well. It's certainly something that's needed now.

In these pages David sets out in a fair and straight-forward way what the policy issues are in the referendum for voters to consider. From migration, trade and sovereignty through to security, education, employment and the environment, voters wanting a digestible summary of the arguments will be glad to have this resource.

He also covers some of the standard questions citizens raise – how does it all work, what is the cost, who is on what side and how did we get to this point. A very useful inclusion is an assessment of the referendum from the perspective of Scotland, Wales and Northern Ireland – often left out of the Westminster narrative.

As he notes, this will only be the third time that a referendum will take place across the whole UK, so it is critical that people feel able to participate in an informed way. Unlike our antiquated Westminster voting system, where millions of voters marooned in 'safe seats' play little role in the final outcome, here is a poll in which – whether cast to Leave or Remain – every vote counts.

So it's vital that people do go out and exercise their democratic right on 23 June. This is a potentially once in a lifetime decision, and one that will shape the next few decades in almost every way possible; economically, politically, and constitutionally. Such a major democratic choice is one that shouldn't be taken lightly – hence the need for resources like these – but it is one that should be taken nonetheless, particularly in the context of the huge instabilities and uncertainties the 21st century has faced so far and which Britain will face – as part of Europe or outside of it – in the coming years.

What next? The Electoral Reform Society has created an online democratic tool to facilitate grassroots discussion about the issues in the referendum. We want voters to read books like David Torrance's and then get together in their communities to debate and learn from each other, so that as we wait for the ballots to be counted following the poll on 23 June we can say that, regardless of the outcome, the campaign has made democracy across the United Kingdom stronger.

EU member countries

- ■ EU country
- ■ non-EU country

1	Denmark
2	The Netherlands
3	Belgium
4	Luxembourg
5	Slovenia
6	Malta
7	Cyprus

The Referendum

On 20 February David Cameron, the Prime Minister, set 23 June 2016 as the date for a referendum on the United Kingdom's membership of the European Union. On that day, voters will be asked the following question in a nation-wide ballot:

> **Should the United Kingdom remain a member of the European Union, or leave the European Union?**

'This is perhaps the most important decision', commented Mr Cameron, 'the British people will have to take at the ballot box in our lifetimes.' His Government had originally planned a straightforward 'Yes' or 'No' referendum, similar to that held on Scottish independence in September 2014, but the Electoral Commission (which regulates elections and referendums in the UK) believed this wording might be leading – or biased – and asked for it to be changed to 'Remain' and 'Leave'.

The First Ministers of Scotland, Wales and Northern Ireland formally objected to the proposed June date, arguing that it came too soon after elections to their devolved assemblies and parliaments in May 2016, but the Prime Minister said he believed the two campaigns could comfortably co-exist. Mr Cameron also made it clear that members of his Government (and individual Conservative MPs) would be free to campaign on both sides of the referendum, and soon after he announced the referendum date Cabinet members began declaring in favour of Leave or Remain.

1

The possibility of holding another referendum on the UK's membership of the EU (the first having been held in June 1975) had been raised over several decades, not least because it has changed significantly since the UK first joined in 1973, with many more members and a far greater number of shared competencies. Over the past 20 years Prime Ministers Tony Blair, Gordon Brown and David Cameron all promised to hold referendums on new EU treaties but later changed their minds, infuriating those who wanted to cast their verdict. A ballot was finally proposed, however, by Mr Cameron during a speech at Bloomberg's London HQ in January 2013. He promised that if the Conservatives were re-elected at the May 2015 general election then he would 'renegotiate' the UK's membership and hold an 'in/out' referendum by the end of 2017.

When the Conservatives won a majority at that election, MPs soon debated and passed the European Union Referendum Act 2015, which enables the referendum to take place on 23 June. It will be only the third such ballot to take place across the whole UK, the first having been in 1975 and the second in 2011 on switching to the Alternative Vote for elections to the House of Commons. Voters in the British Overseas Territory of Gibraltar will also vote in this referendum, as they are subject to full EU membership. Although EU citizens resident in the UK cannot vote in the referendum (except citizens of Ireland, Malta and Cyprus), UK citizens resident in other EU Member States can (as long as they have been resident overseas for less than 15 years), as can citizens of the Commonwealth or British Overseas Territories (like Bermuda and the Falklands) based in the UK or Gibraltar, provided they are old enough and on the electoral register. Citizens of

Jersey, Guernsey and the Isle of Man, however, will not take part, as those British Crown Dependencies are not formally part of the EU.

The Electoral Commission will also regulate campaigning activity before 23 June. By 15 April it will designate which Leave group (Vote Leave or Grassroots Out) will be the 'lead campaigner' on the basis of how much cross-party support each enjoys, as well as campaign tactics and organisational capacity. Its counterpart on the Remain side will almost certainly be the cross-party Britain Stronger in Europe group. There will be strict guidelines for campaign finance, including guidance covering donations and spending, but the lead campaigners on either side will be able to spend £7 million on campaigning, gain access to television and radio airtime, mail-shots and receive a publicly-funded grant of up to £600,000.

The official referendum campaign begins on 15 April 2016, and on polling day there will be 382 local voting areas grouped into 12 regional counts, each of which will have a separate declaration. The Chief Counting Officer will be Electoral Commission Chair Jenny Watson, who will announce the overall referendum result (combining the 12 regional counts and that in Gibraltar) in Manchester Town Hall on Friday 24 June 2016. A simple majority of the total vote is required to provide a winning result, for the UK to either 'Remain' part of or 'Leave' the European Union.

The Renegotiation

2

Following a two-day meeting of the European Council in Brussels, on 19 February 2016 the Prime Minister announced he had reached a deal with the other 27 Member States of the European Union that would form the basis of a referendum to be held on 23 June. David Cameron said the terms dealt with many of the 'frustrations' the British public had with the EU, while critics said the final deal fell well short of what the Prime Minister originally promised when he announced his plan for an EU referendum in early 2013.

Nevertheless, the key elements of the deal were:

- EU migrants' in-work benefits will be 'phased in' over a four-year period if there exist 'exceptional' levels of migration, which the European Commission has confirmed is a condition the UK meets. The UK will be able to operate this 'emergency brake' for seven years, although the details of how this works in practice are still to be confirmed.

- Child benefit for the children of EU migrants living overseas will now be paid at a rate based on the cost of living in their home country: applicable immediately for new arrivals, and from 2020 for the 34,000 existing claimants.

- In due course, EU Treaties will be amended to state explicitly that references to the requirement to seek 'ever-closer union' between Member States 'do not apply to the United Kingdom'.

- A 'red card' system under which 'more than 55 per cent' of national parliaments, or 16 Member States, can ask the European Council to reconsider legislative proposals on grounds of 'subsidiarity'. But the Council can still proceed if it accommodates these concerns.

- The ability for the UK to enact 'an emergency safeguard' to protect the City of London, preventing British firms from being forced to relocate to the Continent and to ensure they do not face 'discrimination' for being outside the Eurozone.

The Prime Minster, however, had to compromise on certain demands in order to get agreement from other EU members. For example, he had originally wanted a complete ban on migrants sending UK child benefit abroad but had to accept a modified arrangement after some eastern European states objected. He also had to shorten the period of the 'emergency brake' from 13 to four years, and accept benefits being phased in rather than removed completely. And while the renegotiation was signed off at the European Council meeting in Brussels, it will still require assent from the European Parliament. It is also not clear if the 'red card' system for national parliaments will ever be triggered in practice.

'The British people must now decide whether to stay in this reformed European Union or to leave,' David Cameron said after the Council meeting. 'This will be a once-in-a-generation moment to shape the destiny of our country.' But before we look at how the EU works and some of the issues likely to be involved in the referendum campaign, let us first look back at the history of the UK's involvement in the European Union.

A Short History of Britain in Europe

3

We must build a kind of United States of Europe. In this way only will hundreds of millions of toilers be able to regain the simple joys and hopes which make life worth living. The structure of the United States of Europe, if well and truly built, will be such as to make the material strength of a single state less important. Small nations will count as much as large ones and gain their honour by their contribution to the common cause.

Winston Churchill, Zurich, 1946

On New Year's Day 1973 the United Kingdom of Great Britain and Northern Ireland joined what was then known as the European Economic Community (EEC), or 'Common Market'. Two years later, in June 1975, the UK's first nation-wide referendum confirmed its membership, and now, more than 41 years later, voters will again endorse or reject continuing membership of a Union that now comprises 28 members rather than the original six.

Back in 1973, Ireland and Denmark also joined the UK in becoming members of the EEC, bringing its total number of Member States to just nine. At midnight on 31 December 1972, a Union flag was raised at the Community's headquarters in Brussels to mark the UK's accession. The then Prime Minister,

Edward Heath, said British membership would lead to 'a great cross-fertilisation of knowledge and information', enabling the UK 'to be more efficient and more competitive in gaining more markets not only in Europe but in the rest of the world'.

Since the Second World War, however, the UK's relationship with the European project had been a troubled and divisive one: when the European Coal and Steel Community was formed in 1951, the UK stood aloof, later declining an invitation to join 'the Six' founding nations of the EEC in 1957, baffling the leaders of France and Germany who well remembered Winston Churchill's 1946 speech calling for a 'United States of Europe'.

And if the UK's view of Europe was ambivalent, some of 'the Six' were ambivalent in return. When Britain changed its mind in the early 1960s and decided to apply for membership of the EEC it was twice vetoed by the French President Charles de Gaulle, who accused the UK of 'deep-seated hostility' towards the European ideal, and of being more interested in links with the United States. And even after the UK's third application was accepted in 1973 (and confirmed in 1975), the debate continued.

Politically, the situation in the mid-to-late 1970s was the reverse of that in 2016: the Labour Party was deeply divided over Europe while the Conservatives (led by Margaret Thatcher) were generally in favour. In Scotland, the SNP had campaigned against continuing membership at the 1975 referendum, as had Plaid Cymru in Wales, while in Northern Ireland both Nationalists and Unionists were split; the SDLP and Vanguard in favour of staying, and the DUP, Sinn Fein and most of the Ulster Unionists in favour of pulling out. In 1975 Scotland was one of the most Eurosceptic parts of the UK, in 2016 it is one of the least.

Europe was also one of the factors that caused Labour to split in 1981, with many on its pro-European wing leaving to form the Social Democratic Party (SDP). For the Conservatives too there were ructions, with Mrs Thatcher, Prime Minister since 1979, becoming rhetorically more hostile. In 1984, for example, she demanded a permanent 'rebate' for the UK on its contributions to what was now known as the European Community (EC). While the French socialist Jacques Delors steered the European Commission towards a more federal Union and a single currency, Mrs Thatcher rejected what she called 'a European super-state exercising a new dominance from Brussels'.

Yet while the 1988 'Bruges speech', from which those words are taken, became a seminal text for Conservative Eurosceptics, it also expressed a continuing commitment to membership of the EC; Mrs Thatcher simply differed as to what form it should take. In 1985 she had signed the Single European Act (partly designed by Lord Cockfield, one of the UK's Commissioners), which further deepened the political and institutional aspect of the EC. By the end of 1990, however, internal Conservative divisions over Europe had contributed to her demise as party leader and Prime Minister.

John Major, Mrs Thatcher's successor, also had his share of European woes, with the UK's forced withdrawal from the Exchange Rate Mechanism (ERM) in September 1992 and subsequent backbench rebellions over the Maastricht Treaty, which involved a further transfer of power from Member States to the rechristened European Union (EU). Major did secure 'opt-outs' from the single currency and new 'Social Chapter' (a package of workers' rights intended to balance the free-market aspect of the EU) but many of his MPs remained sceptical, fearing that the sovereignty of Westminster was being further undermined. The EU, meanwhile, began expanding to include formerly Communist states in Eastern Europe, a process encouraged by the Conservatives and, later, the Labour Party.

With the election of Tony Blair as Prime Minister in 1997, the UK's relationship with the EU seemed to enter a more stable, politically harmonious period. He addressed the European Parliament (as well as France's National Assembly – in French) and reversed his predecessor's opposition to the Social Chapter, delivering social and employment protections long coveted by his party, while also setting his sights on membership of the single currency. But with the economy doing well and limited public support for the Euro, Blair's promised referendum on its adoption never took place.

And although David Cameron had once urged his party to stop 'banging on about Europe', as Prime Minister after 2010 he had little choice, the Conservative Party was once again split over the Europe issue. As party leader he had withdrawn his Members of the European Parliament from the European People's Party, the main centre-right grouping, and subsequently became the first British premier to 'block' a new European Treaty, claiming it put the City of London at risk. The Euro crisis, meanwhile, further diminished the likelihood of the UK joining a troubled single currency.

Parliament also passed the 2011 European Union Act, which required any EU-wide treaty passing substantive new powers to Brussels to be put to British voters in a referendum, while the Government reviewed the 'balance of competences' (or powers) between the EU and Member States in several areas. This concluded that the present balance was about right and did not receive much media attention.

An added factor during this period was the rise of the United Kingdom Independence Party (UKIP), which advocated withdrawal from the EU. UKIP grew steadily, polling just 1 per cent of the UK vote at elections to the European Parliament in 1994, but rising to 6.7 per cent and three MEPs in 1999, more than 16 per cent and around a dozen representatives in 2004 and 2009, and in 2014 becoming the largest UK party with 27.5 per cent (more than 4,376,000 votes) and 24 MEPs. It struggled, however, in Westminster elections, winning its first MP in 2015 having gained two defectees from the Conservatives in the preceding months. Nevertheless, increasing support for UKIP worried many Conservatives and put further pressure on the Prime Minister to appear more Eurosceptic.

Finally, at the beginning of 2013, Mr Cameron promised a referendum on the UK's membership of the EU, pledging to 'renegotiate' its terms, just as his Labour predecessor Harold Wilson had done back in 1975. The Prime Minister was confident of drawing a line under that long-running issue, just as he had tried to do with Scotland in the autumn of 2014. But he did so during challenging economic circumstances and in the midst of a migrant crisis impacting on several other European Member States.

So the European question remained an ambivalent one. Even proponents of continued membership acknowledged that the EU was not perfect, while the Prime Minister sought to reassure voters that if they did decide to Remain then the UK would enjoy a 'special status' in the Brussels-based Union.

3

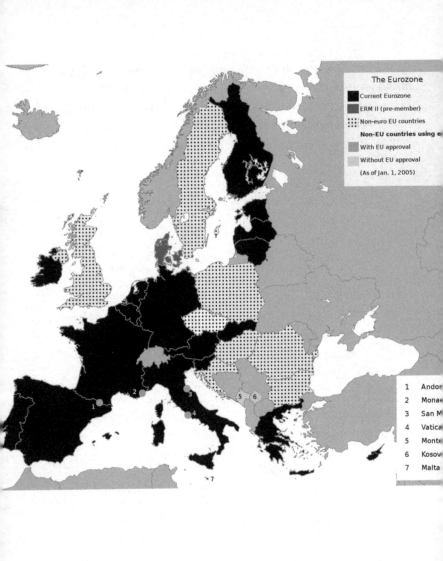

The Eurozone

- Current Eurozone
- ERM II (pre-member)
- Non-euro EU countries
- **Non-EU countries using e**
- With EU approval
- Without EU approval

(As of Jan. 1, 2005)

1 Andor
2 Mona
3 San M
4 Vatica
5 Monte
6 Kosov
7 Malta

How does the
European Union work?

The European Union (EU) is a political and economic organisation with 28 'Member States' and a population of more than 508 million people. Although each of the 28 countries that belong to the Union are all independent (or 'sovereign') countries, they have chosen to 'pool' some of that sovereignty, so that each Member State delegates aspects of its decision-making ability (or 'competences') to the shared institutions of the EU. This means that it is neither a fully federal system like the United States, nor a looser co-operative body like the United Nations – indeed it is not a 'state' at all.*

A 'Single Market' for goods, services, capital and workers (its 'four freedoms') lies at the heart of the EU, with its 'citizens' free to live and work wherever they wish, many (but not all) of them using a single European currency called the Euro. Like most political institutions the EU is based on the rule of law, its actions determined by 'Treaties' agreed and signed by all

* The EU also has nine 'Outermost Regions' (OMR), that is territories belonging to Member States but not geographically part of Europe (for example the Canary Islands, which are Spanish but located off the west coast of Africa). Nevertheless, EU law applies automatically to these territories and some use the single currency. In addition, there more than 20 'Overseas Countries and Territories' (OCT) that have a special relationship with either Denmark, France, the Netherlands and the UK (for example the Falklands), all EU Member States. EU law does not apply to those, although OCTs are entitled to ask for EU financial support.

Member State governments and usually applied domestically following ratification by national parliaments (or via a referendum). These set out the objectives of the EU, rules for its institutions and how future decisions are to be made. The Treaties and activities of the EU are generally under the legal jurisdiction of the European Court of Justice. The most recent – the Lisbon Treaty – came into force on 1 December 2009.

Decision-making at EU level involves various European procedures and institutions, including:

The European Commission

This is the executive arm of the EU and comprises a Brussels-based 'college' of 28 Commissioners, one from each Member State. It proposes legislation, policies and programmes of action and is responsible for implementing the decisions of the European Parliament and the Council. It also represents the Union to the outside world with the exception of the Common Foreign and Security Policy (which falls to the European Council and Council of Ministers). Appointed every five years, Jean-Claude Juncker is the current President of the European Commission (the British politician Roy Jenkins was President between 1977 and 1981) and the UK's present Commissioner is Lord Hill, who is responsible for financial services and markets. The Commission has offices in London, Edinburgh, Cardiff and Belfast, although the UK is under-represented in terms of staff based at its 'Berlaymont' HQ in Brussels.

The European Council

The European Council, which meets at least four times a year, brings together the EU's heads of state and government, ie Presidents and Prime Ministers, along with its own President

(Donald Tusk), the High Representative for Foreign Affairs and Security Policy (Federica Mogherini) and the President of the European Commission (Juncker). It gives the EU political direction (decided by consensus) but does not legislate. There are also related meetings called 'Euro summits', although the UK does not take part in those, as they only concern the single currency.

Council of the European Union

Also known as the Council of Ministers or simply 'the Council', this is attended by one minister from each of the EU's Member States, who then discuss, agree, amend and, finally, adopt legislation (in conjunction with the European Parliament, known as 'co-decision') concerning economic and foreign policy, as well as the EU's budget (again, in conjunction with the European Parliament). The Presidency of the Council (which is not the same as the President of the European Council) rotates between the Member States every six months. The UK is due to assume the presidency in the second half of 2017 (having also held it during 1977, 1981, 1986, 1992, 1998 and 2005). There are also sub-Council 'configurations', for example EU finance ministers collectively form the Economic and Financial Affairs (Ecofin) Council.

Votes in the Council are quite complex, but all "Acts" require at least 258 votes, cast by a majority of members, to be adopted (where a Treaty requires them to be adopted on a proposal from the Commission). In other cases, Acts of the Council require at least 258 votes in favour cast by at least two-thirds of the members in order to pass. When a decision is to be adopted under the 'Qualified Majority Voting' (QMV) procedure, a member of the Council may request verification that the Member States constituting the qualified majority represent at least 62 per cent of the total population of the Union. If that condition is shown not to have been met, then the decision in question will not be adopted. QMV allocates votes to Member States in part according to their population, but is heavily weighted in favour of smaller countries.

The European Parliament

This is the directly-elected arm of the EU, with 751 Members of the European Parliament (MEPs) elected every five years by 28 Member States. Officially located in Strasbourg and Brussels (moving between the two parliament buildings costs 180 million euros a year), it also has an administrative base in Luxembourg. The European Parliament has three main roles: 1) sharing the power to legislate with the Council of Ministers, 2) exercising democratic scrutiny of all EU institutions (it can approve or reject the nomination of the Commission President and other Commissioners, but only as a block), and 3) shared authority with the Council of Ministers over the EU budget.

MEPs do not sit in national delegations but in cross-national political groups, the main centre-right grouping being the European People's Party (EPP) and the predominant centre-left alliance being the Party of European Socialists (PES). There are also groups called the Alliance of Liberals and Democrats for Europe (ALDE), Greens/European Free Alliance (EFA), and several others.

The UK has 73 MEPs and is divided into 12 electoral regions comprising the nations and regions of the UK. Each region has between three and 10 MEPs as follows: Eastern (7), East

Midlands (5), London (8), North East (3), North West (8), South East (10), South West (6), West Midlands (7), Yorkshire and Humber (6), Wales (4), Scotland (6) and Northern Ireland (3). The British Overseas Territory of Gibraltar forms part of the South West region, while the European Parliament has offices in London and Edinburgh. Lord Plumb, a British MEP, was President of the European Parliament from 1987 to 1989.

In recent years the UK's representation in the European Parliament has been reduced due to the addition of more Member States, and critics argue that it is politically weak, wasteful (its expenses system regularly generates negative media stories) and suffers from having a low profile among British voters.

Legislative procedure

Although the European Council determines the general political direction and priorities of the EU, it does not possess legislative functions. Rather it is the European Commission that proposes new laws and the European Parliament and European Council that adopt them. EU 'regulations' have binding legal force throughout every Member State and enter into force on a set date, while EU 'directives' lay down certain results that must be achieved, although each Member State is free to decide how to transpose them into their national law.

While the Commission-Council-Parliament triumvirate is the most important when it comes to legislation, the European Economic and Social Committee (representing employers and trades unions) and the Committee of the Regions (the voice of local and regional government) also have to be consulted (see below). One million EU citizens (from at least seven Member

States) can also invite the Commission to bring forward a legislative proposal via a 'European Citizens' Initiative', although to date none have been successful.

National parliaments

The 2009 Lisbon Treaty clarified the rights and duties of Member States' parliaments within the EU. National parliaments can give a 'reasoned opinion' on a legislative proposal from the European Commission if they believe it does not comply with the principle of 'subsidiarity', under which decisions are taken, according to the Maastricht Treaty, 'as closely as possible to the citizens'. Depending on the number of reasoned opinions, the Commission may have to re-examine its proposal and decide whether to maintain, adjust or withdraw it. This is referred to as the 'yellow' and 'orange card' procedure. A more robust 'red card' procedure, whereby a majority of national parliaments could block EU legislation, has been proposed but not yet adopted.

United Kingdom Permanent Representation to the European Union (UKRep)

This represents the UK in negotiations that take place in the EU, comprising a team sourced from more than 20 UK Government departments working, according to its website, 'to ensure that UK policies are explained to other EU Member States, the European Commission and members of the European Parliament'. Ivan Rogers is the UK's Permanent Representative to the EU and has overall responsibility for the work of the mission, representing the UK at weekly Committee of Permanent Representatives (Coreper II) meetings in the Council of the European Union.

The Court of Justice of the European Union

The Court of Justice of the European Union comprises one Judge from each Member State and eight 'Advocates General', and ensures that legislation is interpreted and applied in the same way across the EU. To this end, the Court checks the legality of the actions of the EU institutions, ensures that Member States comply with their obligations, and interprets EU law at the request of national courts. Lord Mackenzie-Stuart, a Scottish lawyer, was President of the European Court from 1984–88.

The Council of Europe

This is not actually an EU institution at all, but an inter-governmental organisation aiming to protect human rights, democracy and the rule of law. It was set up in 1949 and later drew up the European Convention on Human Rights (ECHR), and, to enable citizens to exercise their rights under that Convention, it also set up the European Court of Human Rights. The Council of Europe has 47 Member States, including all EU countries, and is based in Strasbourg.

The European External Action Service

Relations with countries not in the EU are the responsibility of the High Representative of the Union for Foreign Affairs and Security Policy, who is appointed by the European Council and puts into effect Common Foreign and Security Policy (CFSP) decisions made by the European Council and Council (of Ministers). The European External Action Service (EEAS) serves as a foreign ministry and diplomatic service for the Union under the authority of the High Representative, while the European Commission handles humanitarian and development

ECHR Ratification by
decade
- 1950s
- 1960s
- 1970s
- 1980s
- 1990s
- 2000s

aid for non-EU countries. In 2014, for example, £1.14 billion of the UK's £11.73 billion aid budget was managed through the European Commission, also counting towards its target of spending 0.7 per cent of GDP on international aid.

The European Economic and Social Committee

The European Economic and Social Committee (EESC) is an advisory body of the EU comprising civil society represen-tatives from socioeconomic, civic, professional and cultural areas. They deliver 'opinions' to the European Commission, Council and the European Parliament, acting as a bridge between EU institutions and EU citizens. The UK has 24 members.

4

The Committee of the Regions

The Committee of the Regions (CoR) is another advisory body composed of representatives from Europe's regional and local authorities, giving those institutions a say in EU policymaking. All UK members of the CoR are elected politicians representing local authorities or the devolved legislatures of Scotland, Wales, Northern Ireland and London (Scotland, for example, has 8 members: 4 councillors and 4 Members of the Scottish Parliament). The Local Government Association (LGA) acts as a secretariat for the UK's Delegation, which is led by Councillor Paul Watson, the leader of Sunderland Council. Both the CoR and EESC, however, have limited influence within the institutions of the EU, and especially compared with the Commission, Council and Parliament.

Economic and Monetary Union

Economic and Monetary Union (EMU) is a core element of European integration and all EU Member States are involved.

Although fiscal policy (taxation and spending) remains the responsibility of individual countries, public finances and structural policies are co-ordinated across the EU, although naturally much more closely between countries within the single currency Eurozone.

The European Central Bank

The European Central Bank (ECB) exists to maintain monetary stability in the Eurozone area by ensuring low and stable consumer price inflation. It is independent from other EU institutions, but the UK is not covered by its remit.

The European Investment Bank and Investment Fund

The European Investment Bank (EIB) is the Bank of the EU, owned by Member States and lending money for investments that support the Union's objectives, for example transport networks, environmental sustainability and innovation. The EIB is the majority shareholder in the European Investment Fund (EIF), which finances investment in small and medium-sized enterprises (SMEs), comprising 99 per cent of EU companies and employing more than 100 million Europeans.

The European Court of Auditors

The European Court of Auditors (ECA) independently audits the EU's income and expenditure, making sure both comply with the law and sound financial management. It is often pointed out that since the mid-1990s the ECA has frequently given an 'adverse opinion' on errors in the EU's accounts and therefore declined to sign them off, although many believe this is because the bar is set too high for it to do so.

The European Ombudsman

An Ombudsman is elected by the European Parliament for a renewable term of five years. He or she receives and investigates complaints, helping to uncover maladministration in EU institutions and other bodies.

The European Data Protection Supervisor

The European Data Protection Supervisor (EDPS) protects personal data gathered by EU institutions.

4

How much does the EU cost?

All Member States make payments for membership of the European Union, which can be broken down into four main areas:

- **Contributions based on each Member State's Gross National Income (GNI)**
- **Customs duties relating to the Single Market**
- **Levies on sugar**
- **Contributions based on Value Added Tax (VAT), a tax (with certain exemptions) on goods and services**

Some Leave campaigners have claimed that membership costs £55 million a day, a figure derived from an Office for National Statistics (ONS) publication, although the ONS says it has been taken out of context, not least because it is a 'gross' figure and does not take into account rebates and grants. Nevertheless, proponents of the UK's withdrawal from the EU argue that this money could be better spent on schools, hospitals and other public services, while those who want to 'Remain' say the daily cost of EU membership is more than outweighed by benefits such as lower prices and investment.

The UK is one of ten Member States which pays more into the EU budget than it gets out, with only France and Germany contributing more. In 2014/15 Poland was the largest beneficiary, followed by Hungary and Greece. In the same financial year EU membership 'cost' the UK £17.8 billion, equivalent to £49 million a day, although that figure has to be set against what the UK *receives* from the EU:

- Since 1984 the UK has received a 'rebate' from the EU, worth £4.9 billion last year. This is applied automatically, so the amount the UK actually paid last year was £12.9 billion, or a daily rate closer to £35 million.

- Around £4.4 billion also flowed back to the UK, mainly via:

a The EU Rural Development Fund, and predominantly the Common Agricultural Policy (CAP), which supports the incomes of British farmers by subsidising food production. This was worth more than £3 billion in 2014–15 (see Chapter 10 for more details).

b The European Social Fund (ESF), which finances programmes in Scotland, Wales, Northern Ireland, England and Gibraltar intended to reduce long-term unemployment. In 2014–15 the UK received more than £428 million.

c The European Regional Development Fund (ERDF); more than £693 million in 2014–15.

d Other EU expenditure, worth nearly £47 million in 2014–15.

e And finally EU payments to the private sector in the UK, including for research, which in 2013 were worth an estimated £1.4 billion.

According to Treasury calculations, this means the UK's 'net' outlay was closer to £8.8 billion last year (nearly double what it was in 2009–10), about £24 million a day or 1.4 per cent of total public spending. Those who want the UK to 'Remain' in the EU argue that is a small price to pay for access to the Single Market and significantly lower than the figure used by Leave campaigners, while those advocating withdrawal point out that even when rebates and grants are taken into account, the UK could still save a lot of money by not contributing anything at all. They point out that since 1973 the UK has contributed nearly £500 billion to the EU, although again that does not take into account rebates and grants.

As the House of Commons Library has observed: 'There is no definitive study of the economic impact of the UK's EU membership or the costs and benefits of withdrawal.' So many of the considerations involved in calculating the economic cost or benefit are 'intangible', but various studies have calculated that the EU benefits the UK to the tune of 2, 2.1, 2.25... and as high as 5 per cent of GDP each year, while another claimed a net cost to consumers of 2.5 per cent. The CBI, meanwhile, estimates that the UK benefits by between £62–78 billion a year. Others, including the European Commission, argue that reducing the EU to a cost-benefit analysis excludes lots of other benefits in terms of security and opportunities for EU citizens to live, study and work in other countries.

One benefit that is possible to quantify is regional aid. The UK actually helped develop this system after joining the EEC in 1973 (Britain's Commissioner, George Thomson, was given responsibility for 'regional policy'), intended to act as a counterbalance to the Common Agricultural Policy while developing poorer parts of Member States. Although the UK now receives less than it once did in 'structural funding' as a consequence of EU expansion, between 2014 and 2020 it will still receive 9.57 billion euros, comprising 457 million euros for Northern Ireland, 795 million euros for Scotland, 2,145 million euros for Wales and 6,174 million euros for England.

The bulk of this spending is concentrated in 'Objective 1' regions, defined as those having a standard of living of less than 75 per cent of the EU average. As some of these regions have prospered (partly as a result of EU assistance), however, they have ceased to be eligible. 'Objective 2' aid, meanwhile, covers areas adjusting to change in industrial and services sectors; rural areas in decline; urban areas in difficulty; and economically depressed areas heavily dependent upon fisheries.

In the UK, parts of Wales and Northern Ireland, as well as Merseyside in England, have all benefitted from this aspect of the EU (projects receiving grants are required to display the European flag). Like most EU schemes, however, regional policy has been criticised as wasteful and inefficient. As Prime Minister, Gordon Brown argued that responsibility ought to be transferred to Member States, or structural funds restricted to EU countries with GDP per head of less than 90 per cent of the EU average. The Welsh Government, for obvious reasons, was strongly opposed.

By withdrawing from the EU the UK could save money: between 2007 and 2013 it paid 36 billion Euros towards regional aid and received only 10.6 billion in return. But if the UK wanted to retain access to the Single Market, it would probably have to continue making a contribution to regional aid, as do Norway and Switzerland, while also coming up with transitional aid for parts of the UK currently in receipt of EU structural funding.

5

The 'Remain' Campaign

The campaign for the UK to 'Remain' in the European Union – also known as the 'In' campaign – is called 'Britain Stronger in Europe' (BSiE), which is chaired by the businessman Lord (Stuart) Rose of Monewden and run by the former Labour candidate Will Straw, son of the former Foreign Secretary Jack Straw. Its board includes political representatives from the Conservatives, Labour, Liberal Democrats and Greens, the nations and regions of the UK, and also others from civic and arts organisations.

BSiE's basic message is that the UK is 'stronger, better off and safer in Europe' than we would be 'out on our own'. And while it acknowledges that the EU 'isn't perfect', it says leaving 'would risk our prosperity, threaten our safety and diminish our influence in the world'. BSiE's website lists the main benefits as being:

- **A stronger economy that delivers opportunity now and for future generations – opportunity through growth, trade, investment, jobs and lower prices.**

- **Stronger leadership on the world stage, enabling us to shape the future – influence through participation.**

- **Stronger security in a dangerous world, keeping Britain safe – safety though partnerships.**

It then fleshes out its arguments on these three key points:

A Stronger Economy

'Being part of Europe makes our economy stronger, helping British businesses small and large, creating jobs for British people, and delivering lower prices for British families. Half of everything we sell to the rest of the world we sell to Europe – and we get an average of £26.5 billion of investment into Britain per year from Europe. That's why the Confederation of British Industry (CBI) estimates that 3 million jobs in Britain are linked to trade with the rest of Europe.

Being part of Europe also means cheaper prices in our supermarkets, cheaper flights to Europe and lower phone charges when travelling. The average person in Britain saves around £450 every year because trading with Europe drives down the price of goods and services.

And we get out more than we put in. Our annual contribution is equivalent to £340 for each household and yet the CBI says that all the trade, investment, jobs and lower prices that come from our economic partnership with Europe is worth £3,000 per year to every household. That's a return on investment of almost ten to one. British families are better off being in Europe.

Negotiating as part of a 500 million-strong economy also gives us clout we could never have on our own. Thanks to our membership of the European Union, we benefit from free trade agreements with 50 countries around the world.

So why would we risk our economic security by turning our backs on Europe? There will be no going back if we vote to leave. And if we do leave, we will be cut off from automatic access to the economic benefits that the EU brings – hitting businesses, risking jobs and threatening families' financial security.'

Stronger Leadership

'If we want Britain to be a leader in the world, we need to be in Europe helping to take the big decisions – not sitting on the sidelines, powerless. In today's complex world, the UK has more control over its destiny by staying inside organisations like the EU. We would never dream of leaving the UN or NATO. Why would we leave the EU?

Being part of Europe means we have stronger leadership on the world stage, enabling us to shape the future – influence through participation.

Britain is not Britain unless we are outward-looking, engaged in our continent and leading in Europe. To leave Europe would mean less influence on the world stage, and less say in the future. We are stronger in Europe than on our own.'

6

Stronger Security

'In today's world, many of the threats to Britain's security are global in nature – like the aggression of Russia, terrorism and cross-border crime. Being in Europe, working with our closest neighbours and partners to tackle these threats, makes Britain safer. Whether it's implementing sanctions against Russia, sharing intelligence about terrorists or arresting criminals using the European Arrest Warrant, there is strength in numbers.

Hussein Osman, a terrorist involved in the attempted bomb attack on London in July 2005, is one of over 400 criminals who have been returned to face justice in Britain under the

European Arrest Warrant after fleeing to Europe. He was caught in Italy, brought back to Britain, and sentenced to 40 years' imprisonment. Leaving Europe would threaten our safety. We are stronger and more secure as part of Europe than on our own.'

Website: **http://www.strongerin.co.uk/**

Other 'In' campaigns
Political parties and other groups are also running their own parallel campaigns for the UK to Remain in the EU.

Labour In for Britain Campaign
The 'Labour In for Britain Campaign' is chaired by the Labour MP and former Home Secretary Alan Johnson. It argues that being in the EU 'brings us jobs, growth and investment', while the EU has helped 'to secure workers' rights and make consumers better off too. Representatives from this campaign are unwilling to campaign alongside the Prime Minister.

Website: **http://www.labour.org.uk/index.php/inforbritain**

Conservatives IN
Run by Charlotte Vere, this Conservative Party group argues that the UK is 'Better Off', 'Safer' and 'Stronger' as part of the EU, while its 'Special Status IN A Reformed European Union' gives it 'The Best Of Both Worlds'.

Website: **http://www.conservatives.in/**

Liberal Democrat #INtogether campaign
The Liberal Democrats believe 'Britain is best when we work with other countries and stand tall in the world'. 'We live in an ever increasing globalised economy where we are always

running to catch up,' its website adds. 'We firmly believe that being a strong member in Europe is in the best interest of our country.'

Website: **http://www.libdems.org.uk/europe-issues**

Another Europe Is Possible

'Another Europe Is Possible' is a campaign for a 'radical "in" vote' in the EU referendum. It wants to build a Europe of 'democracy, human rights, and social justice' and does not believe that leaving the EU 'offers a path towards the social, citizen-led Europe we so urgently need'. It wants to 'stay in Europe to change Europe', breaking 'with the free market economics that have caused so much damage to our societies'.

Website: **http://www.anothereurope.org/**

SNP In Europe campaign

See Chapter 13

The 'Leave' Campaigns

There are two main groups campaigning for the UK to 'Leave' the European Union (or get 'Out'), 'Vote Leave' and 'Grassroots Out' (GO), but only one will be designated the 'official' campaign by the Electoral Commission by 15 April 2016.

Vote Leave

Vote Leave was launched on 9 October 2015 and comprises a cross-party group of MPs and peers from the Conservatives, Labour and UKIP. It is run by the founder of the Taxpayers' Alliance, Matthew Elliot, and Dominic Cummings, a former special adviser to the Conservative Cabinet minister Michael Gove. UKIP's only MP, Douglas Carswell, also supports Vote Leave.

Vote Leave says it is campaigning for the UK to Leave the EU because EU institutions 'cannot cope' with the technological and economic forces 'changing the world fast'. So it wants to negotiate a new UK-EU deal based on 'free trade and friendly cooperation'. Its website continues:

> We end the supremacy of EU law. We regain control. We stop sending £350 million every week to Brussels and instead spend it on our priorities, like the NHS and science research. We regain our seats on international institutions like the World Trade Organisation so we are a more influential force for free trade and international cooperation. A vote to 'leave' and a better, friendlier relationship with the

EU is much safer than giving Brussels more power and money every year.

A document detailing a much longer case for leaving the EU can be found at the Vote Leave website:

https://d3n8a8pro7vhmx.cloudfront.net/voteleave/pages/98/attachments/original/1455376673/website-brochure-hq-10_i.pdf

Three main Eurosceptic groups are also supporting Vote Leave:

- **Conservatives for Britain**. This says it represents 'the large number of Conservative Party supporters who want to see a new relationship between Britain and the EU based on free trade and friendly co-operation, rather than political union'. Its president is the former Chancellor Lord (Nigel) Lawson.

  Website: http://conservativesforbritain.org/

- **Labour Leave**. Although the majority of Labour MPs support continued UK membership, Labour Leave believes that UK public services ought to be 'protected from the provisions of EU free trade deals', while rules governing freedom of movement need to be reformed 'so that they are fair for British workers'.

  Website: http://labourleave.org/

- **Business for Britain**. This exists to 'give a voice to the large, but often silent, majority among Britain's business community who want to see fundamental changes made to the terms of our EU membership'. It has published a 1,030-page report, 'Change or Go: How Britain Would Gain Influence and Prosper Outside an

Unreformed EU', which makes the case for reform and/or withdrawal in more detail (see Chapter 21).

Website: **http://businessforbritain.org/**

Website: **http://www.voteleavetakecontrol.org/**

Grassroots Out (GO)

Grassroots Out, or GO for short, is another umbrella group campaigning for the UK to Leave the EU and was founded by the Conservative MPs Peter Bone and Tom Pursglove and Labour MP Kate Hoey. The group is funded by UKIP donor Arron Banks as well as other business people. It was launched on 23 January 2016 in Kettering, Northamptonshire, at an event featuring speakers from the Conservative Party, Labour, UKIP and the DUP. It aims to bring together the existing Leave campaigns and get 'them to work as one in local areas'. 'We are an organisation that unites people from all political parties, and none, into one effective anti-EU ground campaign,' explains its website, 'which is working towards winning the referendum, door by door, vote by vote.' It is supported by the UKIP leader Nigel Farage and the Respect politician (and former Labour MP) George Galloway.

Website: **http://grassrootsout.co.uk/**

Leave.EU

Backing Grassroots Out is Leave.EU, which says UK membership of the EU is too expensive, while the EU itself, according to its Chief Executive Liz Bilney, is 'run for big business, big banks and big politics – not for ordinary people'. Leave.EU began life as 'The Know' campaign launched in August 2015. On its website it makes the following arguments:

- Imagine having £1,000 more to spend each year. By leaving the EU, each household could be better off by this amount – through cheaper food bills, no membership fees, with the cost of regulations lifted, too.

- Imagine not having our laws dictated to us by Brussels. Instead, MPs would become accountable to the public and we would once again be able to make and decide on our own laws.

- Imagine how we could then regain control of important issues such as our borders. We could welcome the right talent from all over the world – adding to the country's already phenomenal cultural and economic strength (rather than having to accept all EU migrants regardless of skill level).

- Imagine having greater influence over our global trade, so that we can do our own deals with fast-growing Commonwealth countries and North America (without 27 other EU countries all arguing for their own special interests!).

- Imagine the sense of pride we would get from negotiating our own global trade deals; if Iceland can negotiate a free trade deal with China, then we most certainly can.

Website: http://leave.eu/

7

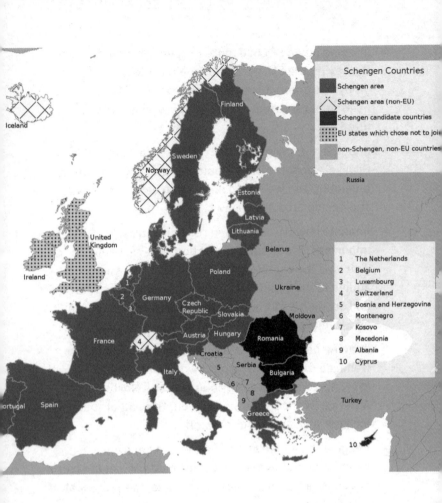

Schengen Countries

- ▇ Schengen area
- ⬚ Schengen area (non-EU)
- ■ Schengen candidate countries
- ⫶ EU states which chose not to join
- ▨ non-Schengen, non-EU countries

1	The Netherlands
2	Belgium
3	Luxembourg
4	Switzerland
5	Bosnia and Herzegovina
6	Montenegro
7	Kosovo
8	Macedonia
9	Albania
10	Cyprus

ean Economic Area Member Countries

■ EEA member countries
■ non-EEA member countries

The Issues – Migration

Migration – whether from within or outside the European Union or European Economic Area (EEA) – is perhaps one of the defining themes of the referendum campaign. Immigration into the UK has consistently been among the public's top five most important issues for a number of years, and often a link to membership of the EU is made in public debate. But a distinction has to be made between migration from the EEA (EU Member States plus Iceland, Norway and Liechtenstein) and non-EEA migration (people coming to the UK from the rest of the world). The UK has much greater control over the latter than the former. Non-EEA migration, for example, increased during the 1990s and early 2000s, but has since declined following a peak in 2004-06.

The two often get conflated, so for example the ongoing migrant crisis, which last year saw more than a million Syrians and North Africans making a perilous journey to Europe, as well as the existence of a 'migrant camp' at Calais in France, was seen by some to increase the number of UK citizens who wanted the UK to leave the EU. But the UK is *not* part of an EU-wide scheme initiated by Germany to settle migrants from outside Europe, having opted out of EU asylum and immigration law via the 1997 Amsterdam Treaty. The UK has, however, offered to take 20,000 over the next five years. The Prime Minister (supported by the French finance minister Emmanuel Macron) has also warned that if the UK left the EU then the Calais camp could relocate to Dover, something

8

Leave campaigners dismiss as 'scaremongering' given that it existed as a result of the bilateral 2003 Le Touquet Treaty rather than EU law.

In terms of migration from the EEA, meanwhile, official figures suggest 257,000 EU citizens came to the UK during 2015 (although 630,000 registered for a National Insurance number in the same period, many staying in the UK for just a few weeks), while a total of around 3 million are resident in the UK. As a member of the EU, the UK must allow citizens of all other 27 Member States to live and work in the country, although the reverse is also true, with around 2 million people from the UK resident in other EU countries.

So if the UK leaves the EU, it would regain the power to stop EEA migrants settling in the country, although restricting their 'freedom of movement' might make it difficult for the UK to negotiate trade deals with the rest of the EU. For example countries outside the EU that have struck free-trade deals with Brussels, such as Norway and Switzerland, have had to allow EU nationals access to their job markets in return.

And there would also be a *quid pro quo* in that citizens of the UK would no longer automatically be able to live and work in countries like Spain and France. Around 5.5 per cent of Ireland's population, for example, was born in the UK, while more than 381,000 UK-born citizens reside in Spain alone. As long as the UK is part of the EU then their pension and healthcare rights are protected under defined reciprocal agreements. NHS treatment is free for those with a European health insurance card and UK state pensioners living in the European Economic Area, but none of these arrangements is certain to survive Brexit.

UKIP wants a five-year ban on permanent settlement by EEA migrants and says outside the EU the UK could adopt an Australian-style 'points' system, which would allow those with skills in short supply in parts of the UK (such as nurses) preferential access to the UK's labour market, as well as temporary 'work permits' for seasonal workers. Although this option is not popular with those who want the UK to 'Remain' part of the EU, opinion polls suggest such restrictions are popular with the general public.

Migrant benefits

A related issue is benefits, the UK Government having talked in the past about what it calls 'benefit tourism', the idea that some EEA migrants settle in the UK purely to take advantage of the Welfare State. At the start of the EU renegotiation process, for example, the Prime Minister said 'we can reduce the flow of people from within the EU by reducing the draw that our welfare system can exert across Europe'.

Quantifying 'benefit tourism', however, is not straightforward; the individual cases of fraud give little evidence of systematic abuse. The UK Government points to Department for Work and Pensions (DWP) figures that show around 40 per cent of all migrants from the EEA are supported by UK benefits, but that has been questioned by the UK Statistics Authority. Other DWP statistics also show that of the 5 million claiming benefits in the UK, 114,000 were EU nationals. Several studies, however, have found that welfare does not tend to 'pull' migrants towards wealthier countries such as the UK, higher wages are more attractive. Vote Leave, for example, believes the UK's new National Living Wage, which starts in April 2016, will be a big 'draw' for EEA migrants.

8

The Prime Minister has said that EEA migrant families coming to the UK could lose an average of £6,000 a year of in-work benefits when his 'emergency brake' is applied. The DWP estimates between 128,700 and 155,100 people would be affected. But UK Government statistics show that recently arrived migrants from Eastern Europe are actually unlikely to claim benefits, the vast majority of claimants having been resident for four or more years and in employment. Another study found that in the decade up to 2011 migrants from the EEA had contributed 34 per cent more in taxes than they had received in benefits. On the other hand, many believe these same migrants have put pressure on public services like schools and hospitals.

A lot of research, however, shows that EEA migrants generally contribute more to UK coffers than they take out, although calculating exactly how much is, as with many other aspects of the EU debate, extremely difficult. On average, however, from 2001–11 those from the EEA are estimated to have contributed £1.34 for every £1 they cost (the same research found those from outside the EU put in £1.02 for every £1 they received). The latest findings, meanwhile, estimate that recent immigrants from the ten countries that joined the EU in 2004 (mainly in Eastern Europe) contributed £1.12 for every £1 received, while those from the rest of the EU put in £1.64 for every £1.

Child benefit
Another bone of contention is the amount of child benefit paid to EEA migrants whose children remain in their home countries, the most recent figures suggesting around £30 million is paid out each year to meet 34,000 claims. So one

element of David Cameron's renegotiation was an agreement that *new* migrants would be paid child benefit at the local rate in their country of origin (a rule to be extended to *existing* claimants after 2020). More widely, migrants will not have full access to UK benefits until four years after their arrival. Critics say none of these measures are likely to significantly reduce levels of migration from the EEA.

Freedom of Movement

Freedom of movement, one of the Single Market's 'four freedoms', means that EU citizens can visit the UK for three months without a visa, six months if seeking a job with a realistic prospect of success, and for an unlimited period to work or study (if self-employed or self-sufficient). The Labour governments of 1997–2010 were generally very relaxed about those coming from the ten new Member States, originally predicted to number between 5–13,000 a year but in fact an average of 170,000 (those staying in the UK for more than 12 months) between 2004 and 2011. When Romania and Bulgaria joined the EU in 2007, the UK imposed restrictions for seven years, but large numbers arrived when those restrictions expired in 2014.

It is important, however, to understand that the UK is *not* part of the 'Schengen Area', the 26 EU and EFTA countries that have abolished passport and other controls at their common, or 'internal', borders. Rather it forms part of the 'Common Travel Area' (CTA), which operates in a similar way for the UK, Ireland, Isle of Man and Channel Islands (Guernsey and Jersey). Schengen came under pressure in 2015 when several Member States reintroduced border controls in a response to the migrant/refugee crisis. Although the EU itself does not issue passports, those issued by the 28 member countries share a common format, a burgundy-coloured cover (except for Croatia) with the title 'European Union' followed by the name of the Member State.

This obviously makes travel between Member States much easier, while some airline operators have argued that the EU has been integral to the success and spread of budget travel over the past two decades.

But while Ryanair's Michael O'Leary wants the UK to 'Remain' in the EU he predicted that Brexit would not be 'the end of the world' and that it alone would not cause UK air fares to rise. Similarly, British Airways said a 'Leave' vote would cause uncertainty but would not have a 'material impact' on its business.

A piece of European legislation called the Denied Boarding Regulation also allows passengers to claim up to €600 in compensation for delays or cancellations on flights that originate in the EU, which would likely be lost if the UK voted to Leave. Outside the EU, meanwhile, the UK could retain access to the European Common Aviation Area (ECAA) if it followed Norway into the EEA, although that could still result in lots of upheaval for airline operators if not their customers (flying is a very competitive market, which might keep costs low even outside the EU).

8

The Issues – Trade

Since the UK joined the 'Common Market' in 1973, trade has been central to the European project. The 1957 Treaty of Rome set out to remove tariffs and other economic barriers between Member States, a process accelerated with the creation of the Single Market in the early 1990s. Those who want the UK to Remain in the EU cite ease of trade as one of their main arguments, while those who want to Leave say there exist considerable trading opportunities in the rest of the world.

The EU, however, is currently the UK's biggest trading partner by far, accounting for 44.6 per cent of UK goods and services exports (£226.7 billion) in 2014 and 53.2 per cent of imports (£288.3 billion). But there is a large trade deficit, with imports *from* EU countries exceeding exports by £77 billion in 2014. Many who want the UK to Remain in the EU claim '50 per cent' of UK exports go to the EU, but that figure was last true was in 2008; since then it has been in decline.

An analysis of official trade figures by Michael Burrage at the London School of Economics showed that while between 1973 amd 1993 UK exports to the EU increased by more than those of leading non-members (such as the United States, Canada and Australia), since then the situation has reversed, even though those countries have to pay tariffs and the UK does not. Advocates of a 'Leave' vote also point to the EU's declining share of global economic activity, from 30 per cent in 1980 to 17 per cent last year.

9

Nevertheless, those campaigning for the UK to Remain in the EU argue that trade with other EU countries would become much more difficult if the UK was to leave. Europe Minister David Lidington says it could take up to a decade for the UK to renegotiate new trade deals following Brexit, while Michael Froman, the US Trade Representative (and a former European Commission official), said it was 'absolutely clear that Britain has a greater voice at the trade table being part of the EU'. Around a third of FTSE 100 chief executives support 'Remain' on that basis, although Vote Leave say that smaller businesses are more likely to support Brexit; a survey by the Zurich insurance company found that 39 per cent of UK small and medium-sized companies wanted to 'Leave' the EU.' The British Chambers of Commerce, meanwhile, says 55 per cent of its members support staying within a reformed EU, as do most business associations such as the Confederation of British Industry (CBI).

The Conservative Cabinet minister Chris Grayling asks the question: 'Does anybody actually think that on the day after Britain leaves the EU, the Germans are going to turn around and say, "We're not going to sell you BMWs any more"?' Both Rolls Royce and BMW, however, have warned of job losses if the UK leaves the EU. BT chairman Sir Mike Rake, a recent CBI president, says there are 'no credible alternatives' to the UK staying in the EU, while Lord Bamford, chairman of JCB, believes an EU exit would allow the UK to negotiate its own trade deals.

Several economists and think tanks tend to agree that the economic pros and cons – between staying in or leaving the EU – balance out, while 'Leave' campaigners say the Union's sluggish growth rates (in contrast to the UK's relatively positive figures) is a good reason to break free and do its own thing. They make the point that outside the EU the UK could negotiate its own free-trade deals not just with the 27 remaining Member States, but with other countries, something it is currently forbidden to do under EU rules. Lord Lawson of Business for Britain, for example, has argued that globalisation renders the EU increasingly obsolete in trading terms.

Conservative Employment Minister Priti Patel argues that free trade need not be dependent upon a Single Market and common rules enforced by the European Court of Justice. On the contrary, she believes EU rules and regulations have 'suffocated' entrepreneurs, citing the case of vacuum cleaner-manufacturer Dyson being 'discriminated' against in order to protect older German makers. Outside the EU, adds Patel, the UK would be able 'to negotiate free trade agreements with the high-growth parts of the world — to do our own deals with India and China, opening up new markets for our entrepreneurs', while investing some of the money saved from EU membership in 'fundamental scientific research to help Britain stay at the cutting edge of the revolutionary developments in fields such as robotics and genetics'.

In response to these arguments, the former Labour MP, Cabinet minister and EU trade commissioner Peter Mandelson said: 'We would be free to negotiate, but who's going to want to negotiate with us?' Like David Lidington, he predicted that negotiations would take years and potentially leave the UK with a worse deal than it currently enjoys inside the EU. Others point out that while non-EU countries like Norway and Switzerland participate in the Single Market, they pay for the

9

privilege while lacking any voice in how that market is run. Sir John Major, the former Conservative Prime Minister, has made a particularly strong warning regarding trade, arguing that the 'Leave' position is 'self-deception to the point of delusion'. 'Their argument is that the EU needs the UK market more than we need theirs, on the basis that – overall – the EU exports more to the UK than we export to them. This is, at best, disingenuous. More bluntly, it is fantasy.'

Those advocating a vote to 'Leave' have different views as to whether the UK should be part of the European Free Trade Association (EFTA) or European Economic Area (EEA) should it leave the EU (see Chapter 16 for more on this). In 2012 UKIP leader Nigel Farage advocated both 'a simple free trade deal' with the EU and a 'Commonwealth Free Trade Area' with 53 other countries. Critics, however, say the Commonwealth lacks coherent trading infrastructure while its members are at different stages of economic development, making such an agreement unrealistic.

Jobs

Advocates of continuing EU membership also insist that thousands of British jobs are heavily tied to the UK's trading links with other European Member States, although trying to calculate precisely how many is difficult. About 15 years ago two studies by South Bank University and the National Institute for Economic and Social Research (NIESR) estimated that 3.45 and 3.2 million jobs respectively were connected with the UK's membership of the EU.

Many senior figures continue to use this figure (3 or 3.5m) even though the research in question is clearly out of date.

More recently (in 2013), however, the organisation British Influence (based on extensive polling by Business for Britain) calculated a figure closer to 1.5 million. Professor Iain Begg, who worked on one of the earlier studies, argues that his findings were taken out of context and that the 'economic plus or minus' of the UK's EU membership when it comes to jobs would likely be 'very small'.

Large numbers of jobs in other EU countries are also linked to their exports to the UK, so this cuts both ways, with the House of Commons Library having calculated in 2011 that 5 million EU jobs might be lost if exports to the UK were disrupted. Those who advocate a 'Leave' vote, meanwhile, say post-Brexit arrangements could minimise any risk to most, if not all, jobs. As in many other areas, it would depend what sort of relationship the UK negotiated with the EU regarding access to the Single Market. The independent fact-checking organization Full Fact, for example, has drawn a distinction between jobs linked with membership of the EU as an *institution* and the EU as an *export market*.

Many workers, of course, currently move between the UK and EU. In terms of transport, although sea and rail travel would not see much of an impact from Brexit, commercial vehicles like heavy-goods lorries operating on the Continent would have to comply with EU rules for driver working hours and rest periods, and could also find themselves subject to fees.

City of London
Brexit would also have an impact on the City of London, one of the largest financial centres in Europe and indeed the world. It is home to hundreds of foreign banks which currently have

access to the Single Market as a result of the UK's membership of the EU. So if the UK was to leave, it would have to renegotiate its terms of access, something that might offer an opportunity – however fleeting – to competing financial centres like those in New York City and Hong Kong internationally, and Dublin and Frankfurt within the EU.

Opinion in the City is divided, with many larger corporations wanting to 'Remain' because of the Single Market, but many smaller firms arguing that London would thrive if it no longer had to comply with EU regulations. Campaigners for a Leave vote also envision London becoming like Singapore or Hong Kong if freed from EU controls, based on its 70 per cent market share of financial services in Europe, accounting 7.9 per cent of UK GDP and 11.5 per cent of tax receipts (£66 billion) in 2013–14. They also point to EU measures such as a proposed cap on bankers' bonuses (of twice their annual salary) as a threat to the City's competitive advantage, although many of its leading figures agree that leaving the Single Market, or having less say in how it is run, would potentially damage the UK's financial sector.

Foreign Direct Investment

The UK is currently the EU's top destination for what is known as Foreign Direct Investment (FDI), accounting for just over 20 per cent of the total in 2014 ($72 billion). Around half of this investment comes from other EU countries, with the UK acting as a 'gateway' for investors to the Single Market, including around £2.6 billion for the UK's car industry. Many German-owned car manufactures in the UK have suggested this investment could be disrupted if the UK leaves the EU, although UKIP has made the point that many made similar warnings when the UK did not join the single currency.

Those who want to 'Leave' the EU point out that FDI is in decline and say the UK is attractive enough to investors to do well on its own; Germany, for example, exports more cars to the UK than it imports. Those who want to 'Remain', however, warn that even minor uncertainty could impact on long-term investment decisions, for business tends to crave stability. If it left the EU, the UK would have to retain links with the Single Market and cross-border trade mechanisms in order to preserve high levels of FDI. But as the House of Commons Library noted, outside the EU 'the UK may be able to establish a regulatory regime more favourable to overseas investors that could offset the effect of its departure'.

Transatlantic Trade and Investment Partnership
Some advocates of Brexit (and also some of those who want to 'Remain') object to something called the Transatlantic Trade and Investment Partnership (TTIP), currently under negotiation between the EU and the United States and which could potentially create the biggest free-trade area in the world. Supporters, including the Prime Minister, say it could make US imports cheaper and boost UK exports to the US by around £10 billion a year, but opponents, including the Labour leader Jeremy Corbyn, fear it will shift power to multi-national corporations, undermine public services (if Member States choose to include them in TTIP's remit, which they might not), lower food standards and impinge upon basic rights. Quitting the EU, however, would mean the UK would not be part of TTIP.

9

Common Agricultural Policy

In 2015 nearly 200,000 UK farmers shared more than £3 billion from the Common Agricultural Policy (CAP), one of the EU's oldest 'common' policies, which basically distributes subsidies and grants to farmers in all 28 Member States. Although popular with those in the farming sector, CAP has gradually taken up a larger share of the EU's budget, nearly 40 per cent in 2015, to which the UK contributed £5.1 billion, a net subsidy of £2 billion.

In the 1980s (and again in 2009) there was much criticism of so-called 'butter mountains' and 'wine lakes' arising as a result of CAP, which referred to farmers producing simply to earn a subsidy rather than to meet market demand, although this was subsequently reformed. In 1996, meanwhile, the European Commission banned the export of any live cattle, beef, veal or products of bovine origin from the UK to other countries in the EU or elsewhere in the world following an outbreak of 'mad cow disease', a restriction that took several years to reverse.

CAP payments are linked to the size of a farm, so bigger landowners tend to get more, leading both Labour and Conservatives politicians in the UK to have proposed phasing out direct payments by 2020, although this was blocked by other Member States. Although leaving the EU would mean no more co-operation with CAP, it would not remove the need for farming subsidies, although the system could be redesigned. British farmers might experience less 'red tape' but also less cash, and even if the UK Government came up with an alternative system of funding it might not prove as generous as that under CAP. The UK also imports two and a

9

half times more from the EU than from the rest of the world, and new tariffs (as a result of leaving the EU) could add costs to imports. Farmers, meanwhile, would have to negotiate new trading deals with the Continent, and as a result food prices for consumers could fluctuate, although opinion is divided as to whether they would go up or down.

Common Fisheries Policy

A Common Fisheries Policy (CFP) was also an early part of the European project, although it was only introduced in the 1970s. In 1970 an attempt was made by the original six Member States to assert the principle of 'free access' to European Community fisheries, which appeared to four new applicants – Denmark, Ireland, Norway and the UK – as if they were trying to settle the issue to their own advantage before new Member States had an opportunity to exert their influence. A last-minute agreement, however, allowed three of the four (Norway chose not to join) to restrict fishing within a six-mile coastal limit to domestic vessels until the end of 1982.

Since then the EU's waters have been open to all fishermen within a 200-mile limit from the Atlantic and North Sea coasts, but within narrower limits in the Mediterranean and Baltic seas. Member States are, however, allowed to retain limits up to 12 miles from their shores, while in the case of the UK fishing in an area beyond 12 miles around the Orkney and Shetland islands (for potentially endangered species) is subject to a system of EU licenses. The CFP has been reformed several times but remains controversial due to a policy of discarding fish that are not subject to EU quotas, meaning that around a million tonnes a year of often edible

9

fish are simply thrown away. This system, however, is being phased out between 2015 and 2019, depending upon species and region.

The UK has the biggest zone with the largest range of species in the EU, and many politicians believe Scotland in particular has suffered as a consequence of EU fishing policy (although broadly pro-EU, the SNP wants to withdraw from the CFP). So if the UK decides to 'Leave' the EU it would regain control – or sovereignty – over its 'Exclusive Economic Zone', which extends 200 miles from the UK coastline. Most fish, however, do not observe national maritime boundaries, so even outside the EU the UK would have to negotiate reciprocal rights and restrictions to neighbouring waters, either inside or outside the EU.

9

The Issues – Sovereignty

'Sovereignty' is another persistent theme of the European debate. In essence, a country like the UK is 'sovereign' when it has the supreme ability to make and enforce decisions about how it is governed. So the UK Parliament could be said to have given up some of its sovereignty when it passed the European Communities Act in 1972, enabling the UK to join the then EEC and requiring its courts to apply the EU's body of law (or 'acquis communautaire'), but on the other hand it still has the 'sovereign' power to repeal that Act if it wants to.

When the UK joined in 1973, Edward Heath, the then Prime Minister, said there was 'no question of any erosion of essential national sovereignty', although that depended how he defined 'essential'. Despite a lot of rhetoric to the contrary, however, most subsequent British premiers ceded more sovereignty to the EU by approving further transfers of power.

Proponents of the UK remaining part of the EU have generally emphasised that sovereignty is either 'shared' or 'pooled' within the EU. Technically, of course, every Member State remains fully sovereign in that they could choose to leave the EU at any time, just as they chose to join it at various points over the past 60 years. Therefore, those who want the UK to 'Leave' the EU tend to think sovereignty is more important than those who want to 'Remain'. The former argue that the UK is not fully free to make decisions in its own interests, while the latter, such as the Prime Minister, point out that

10

sovereignty is relative, and that even outside the EU the UK would have to compromise on decision making, just as it does within other organisations like NATO (which commits its members to mutual defence) and the United Nations (on, for example, climate change and arms treaties).

As David Cameron put it: 'You might feel more sovereign, but if you can't get your businesses access to European markets, if you can't keep your people safe... you're less in charge of your destiny.' On the other hand, the Justice Secretary, Michael Gove, argues that decisions governing the lives of Britons 'should be decided by people we choose and who we can throw out if we want change', which is not possible for as long as some of those decisions are made by the EU. Similarly, many critics of the EU point out that its most powerful institutions (such as the European Commission and Council) are not directly elected, although the same could be said of the UK's monarchy and Upper House of Parliament, the House of Lords.

Gove has also contradicted the Prime Minister's claim that his EU deal is legally binding and irreversible, predicting that it could be unpicked by the European Court of Justice (another minister said it had all the legal force of a washing machine warranty). Number 10, however, says the renegotiation has legal force as an 'irreversible International Law Decision that requires the European Court of Justice to take it into account'. Boris Johnson, the Mayor of London, objects to what he calls the 'judicial activism' of that European Court, although he and others often conflate it with the European Court of Human Rights, which is *not* an EU institution.

10

Part of the Prime Minister's renegotiation, however, sought to reassure those concerned about sovereignty by speaking of the UK as 'a proud, independent country' and claiming to have secured for it a 'special status' within the EU, exempt from Treaty commitments to 'ever-closer union'. He has also promised to enshrine in statute the 'supremacy' of the UK Supreme Court over the European Court of Justice. This, as legal experts have pointed out, is largely symbolic, not only because Westminster already has the power to ignore EU law if it wants to, but also because the sheer volume of legislation from Brussels makes it impractical.

Talking of EU legislation, those in favour of the UK leaving the Union – particularly members of the United Kingdom Independence Party (UKIP) – often claim that 70–80 per cent of UK law either originates in the Council of the EU or from joint decisions with the European Parliament. This claim appears to come from the former German president Roman Herzog's 2007 comment that 84 per cent of his country's laws were made in Brussels, something he said was an 'inappropriate centralisation of powers away from the Member States towards the EU'.

The German Ministry of Justice had compared the number of directives adopted by the Federal Republic of Germany between 1998 and 2004 with domestic legislative acts, while UKIP revised the figure down to 75 per cent, to take account of the UK not being in the Eurozone. That, however, has been criticised as an inexact approach. By contrast, for example, research by the House of Commons Library found that just nine per cent of statutory instruments passed in the UK Parliament between 1998 and 2005 implemented European legislation.

That same paper, however, also suggested that using statutory instruments was not necessarily the best way to assess the influence of EU legislation on the UK, not least because the number of EU regulations could be two or three times the number of EU directives. 'The proportion of EU based laws', it concluded, 'could therefore be as much as 30–40 per cent or more.'

Even more confusingly, the House of Commons Library recently updated its report on the percentage of EU laws affecting the UK. This time it looked at all Acts of Parliament and implementing measures passed in the last 20 years, and concluded that an average of 1.4 per cent of the former and 12.9 per cent of the latter related to the EU, meaning an average of 13.2 per cent of UK instruments during that period were EU-related. Importantly, that average included laws (the 'vast majority') which simply mentioned the EU or defined an EU term for UK purposes, meaning they were predominantly domestic measures.

11 The Issues – Influence, Security and Risk

Influence

The Prime Minister has made British influence on the world stage a key part of the campaign for the UK to Remain in the European Union, arguing that it has far more clout combined with other EU Member States than it would as a 'lone wolf'. As he said in a speech, he did not deny the UK could survive outside the EU, but the question was how it could 'best succeed, how will we maximise our prosperity, our jobs. How will we maximise the investment into our country.'

Mr Cameron also said having been Prime Minister since 2010 had made him more aware of the importance of the UK 'if you want to fix stuff'. He added:

> **Whether it is trying to stop the people smugglers in the Mediterranean, pirates off the coast of Africa, whether it's confronting Iran about the nuclear programme, whether it's trying to get better results in Syria, we gain by sitting round that table with the French, with the Germans, with the Italians getting things done.**

'Leave' campaigners, however, counter that co-operation like that would also be possible outside the EU, and claim that the UK's influence within the EU is exaggerated, not least because it is regularly outvoted on important decisions in the Council of Ministers. They also point to the potentially greater influence the UK could have if it was able to forge relationships – trading and economic – with large economies outside the EU. It would, for example, still be part of NATO, the G8 and G20, while it could take its own place at the World Trade Organisation (the UK is currently represented by the EU).

UKIP's Nigel Farage has also argued that the UK's permanent place on the United Nations Security Council could come under threat from moves to give the EU a seat instead, while pointing to the UK's significant influence in terms of 'soft power' (cultural, linguistic and diplomatic reach), particularly in the Commonwealth. Although a Chinese newspaper memorably observed that the UK was 'not a big power in the eyes of the Chinese. It is just an old European country apt for travel and study', it still has the fifth-highest GDP in the world.

And although the EU undoubtedly occupies a significant presence on the world stage (the US, for example, values the UK's position as a conduit to the rest of the EU), attempts to foster a European 'demos' (or feeling of solidarity) among Member States have not been very successful. There is a European flag (a circle of yellow stars on a blue background), anthem ('Ode to Joy') and 'Europe Day' (9 May), but none seem to have captured the public's imagination. Many of those who want to 'Leave' the EU, meanwhile, believe the UK's 'special relationship' with the US means it has more influence across the Atlantic than it does across the English Channel.

Security

One of the EU's founding aims was to avoid another European war, and few would deny it has been successful in that aim. It also helped ease the transition of 13 former dictatorships – now EU Member States – into democracies since 1980. In recognition of this, in 2012 the EU was awarded the Nobel Peace Prize for advancing the causes of peace, reconciliation, democracy and human rights in Europe. On the other hand, critics have pointed out that while the EU might have avoided another war between its Member States, it did not respond well to conflict beyond its remit, for example the break up of Yugoslavia (and resulting ethnic conflict) in the early 1990s or the Allied response to the Libyan crisis in 2011.

Meanwhile co-operation on the European Arrest Warrant (EWA), is regularly cited by the Prime Minister (and organisations like the Association of Chief Police Officers) as an EU measure that strengthens security not only in the UK but across European Member States. It allows criminals to be arrested and deported in the EU, and between 2009 and 2013 507 suspects were sent to the UK, including 63 for child sex offences, 105 for drug trafficking and 44 for murder, while more than 4,000 suspects were extradited from the UK to other EU states using EAWs. Under the terms of the 2009 Lisbon Treaty, the UK also 'opts-in' to the cross-border law enforcement agency 'Europol' (based in The Hague), which helps combat terrorism, human trafficking, cybercrime, arms and drug smuggling across the EU. (Non-EU countries like Norway and Switzerland, however, also co-operate fully with Europol.)

The UK Government also argues that if Britain leaves the EU then it will be less protected against external threats, such as Vladimir Putin's Russia, because potential enemies are intimidated by the unity of the 28-strong EU (although that did not make a difference when it came to the Crimean region of

Ukraine, now under Russian control). The Prime Minister has spoken of a potentially greater threat from 'Putin to the East, ISIL/Daesh to the south', Somali pirates and a nuclear Iran.

'Leave' campaigners, however, counter this argument by highlighting the security risks presented by weak or ineffective border controls, citing as an example those who used fake Greek passports to enter Europe and later took part in the Paris terror attacks (one of the attackers had also visited Birmingham). The Work and Pensions Secretary Iain Duncan Smith has even suggested that remaining in the EU could lead to more 'Paris-style' incidents should Syrian or Pakistani extremist asylum seekers acquire EU residency and enter the UK.

In a letter to the *Daily Telegraph* in February 2016, 13 former Armed Forces chiefs said they believed 'strongly that it is in our national interest to remain an EU member' so the UK could protect itself from 'grave security threats' caused by ISIL and Russia. Signatories included Field Marshals Lord Erwin Bramall and Lord Charles Guthrie, although General Sir Michael Rose asked for his name to be removed from the letter, Downing Street blaming his inclusion on an 'administrative error'.

Risk

Those who want the UK to Remain in the UK say that leaving would constitute a 'leap in the dark' and that only the status quo offers stability and consistency, adding that the UK risked being cut off by its former EU partners when it comes to international co-operation and trade. 'Leave' campaigners, on the other hand, say the UK is risking its future by remaining part of an EU that is in economic decline and under pressure from the migrant crisis. The Legatum Institute's World Prosperity League, for example, shows that Norway and Switzerland rank numbers one and two, and both are outside the EU, although Denmark (which is in the EU) is at number three.

Moody's rating agency has underlined the 'Remain' position by predicting that the UK would end up with a negative credit rating if it leaves the EU, while the Swiss bank UBS says the British pound (sterling) would also be hit hard, perhaps ending up on a par with the Euro, which would help UK exporters but make journeys to the Continent much more expensive. The UK Government has also published a 'dossier' warning that Brexit could lead to 'a decade of uncertainty', while Bank of England governor Mark Carney said the possibility of the UK leaving the EU represented the 'biggest domestic risk to financial stability', although he added that remaining in the EU also carried risks.

'Leave' campaigners tend to respond by saying that such claims are deliberately exaggerated, unlikely or constitute 'scaremongering', what some call 'Project Fear'. David Cameron has rejected this, saying he is only interested in 'Project Fact', which is about saying 'stay in and you know what you'll get'. Work and Pensions Secretary Iain Duncan Smith has attacked what he calls the 'spin, smears and threats' of 'Remain' campaigners trying to 'bully' Britons into voting to stay in the EU, while the former Conservative Cabinet minister Liam Fox has said that those who wish to remain in the EU 'should make the positive case for the supranational European project rather than frightening people'.

A distinction should be drawn, however, between baseless scaremongering and the legitimate highlighting of potential risk. For example, Culture Secretary John Whittingdale, who supports 'Leave', says he is not 'going to pretend that there aren't potentially some costs... that there aren't uncertainties' associated with the UK leaving the EU. Foreign Secretary Phillip Hammond has also raised that he sees it as a risk that if the UK leaves, other Member States might ask: 'Well, if the Brits can do it, why can't we?'

The Issues – Employment, Education and Environment

12

Employment

The years following the signing of the Maastricht Treaty saw the introduction of a number of European directives relating to employment, for example agreements that guarantee the right to parental leave, rights for part-time, fixed-term and agency workers, a maximum 48-hour working week (without overtime), paid holiday entitlement, smoke-free workplaces and rights for workers being transferred between jobs (known as 'TUPE' in the UK). There are also social protections such as the right not to be discriminated against on the basis of age, gender, religion, disability, sexual orientation, race or ethnicity. All these, as well as other political, social and economic rights, were enshrined in EU law via the Charter of Fundamental Rights of the European Union, proclaimed in 2000 and taking full legal effect through the Lisbon Treaty of 2009 (some Brexiters, however, claim a protocol exempts the UK).

So leaving the EU would mean that the UK would be able to amend or repeal some of these regulations, something that is difficult to do as a Member State. In the past, for example, the Institute of Directors has identified the Agency Workers Directive (AWD) and the Information and Consultation of Employees Directive as candidates for abolition, as well as amendment of equality laws, TUPE and the Collective Redundancies Directive. A few years ago the Federation of

Small Businesses (FSB) also pointed to the AWD and regulations on self-employed drivers' working time and temporary agency workers as burdens on small businesses and in need of reform. According to the Open Europe think tank, the Working Time Directive costs the UK £4.2 billion a year and the AWD £2.1 billion.

However, even if the UK left the EU a lot of European employment directives would remain in place, having been transposed into employment contracts and company policy, for example maternity leave and holiday entitlement. Leaving the EU would also not necessarily involve ceasing involvement in the European Court of Human Rights, a separate entity to which the UK is committed as a consequence of having signed the European Convention on Human Rights. This has implications when it comes to equality and discrimination, although the UK Government has raised the prospect of introducing a UK Bill of Rights instead. But the European Court of Justice (ECJ) *is* an EU institution, and if the UK withdrew then the UK Supreme Court would be left as the ultimate arbiter of employment law, which could lead to potential differentiation between workers' rights in different parts of Europe.

Some of those who want the UK to Leave the EU argue that repealing European employment regulations would make the UK more competitive – a 2011 report from the think tank Open Europe having calculated that full deregulation of EU social policy regulations 'would yield an annual £14.8 billion boost to UK GDP'. But at the same time the same regulations are in place across the EU, designed to create a level playing field and protect employees. The former Conservative Party leader

Michael Howard, who backs 'Leave', has said that even outside the EU, if the UK was trading with other European countries then 'one aspect of that must be [that] you don't undercut each other on the basis of poor terms and conditions. That's an essential part of being in Europe.'

As well as protection for employees, European legislation also offers certain safeguards for consumers, intended to harmonise their rights across the EU. One significant example relates to the cost of using a mobile phone outside the UK. The resulting 'roaming charges' used to be very expensive, but in the summer of 2015 the European Commission agreed on Single Market legislation for telecoms, meaning that tourists in EU countries would pay the same mobile fees as in their home country. The additional charges for using a mobile abroad will therefore reduce from April 2016 and disappear completely from June 2017, significantly lowering bills. Outside the EU the UK may no longer necessarily be covered by this incoming regulation, although it is possible that once in place, mobile phone operators will be reluctant to reverse the changes for fear of losing customers.

Education

Under the laws governing freedom of movement, EU citizens moving from one Member State to another have the same access to education as domestic nationals. Similarly, every eligible EU student pays the same tuition fees – and can apply for some of the same student support – as nationals of the hosting EU country (although because EU rules allow discrimination *within* a Member State, EU citizens do not pay fees in Scotland while those from the rest of the UK do).

In 2013–14, there were 125,300 EU students at UK universities resulting in payments of £224 million in fee loans to EU students on full-time courses in England. Since 1987 the UK's membership of the EU has also provided British students with educational opportunities via the Erasmus Programme ('European Region Action Scheme for the Mobility of University Students'), a student-exchange programme named after the Dutch theologian. Since January 2014 this has been known as Erasmus Plus, which combines all the EU's current schemes for education, training, youth and sport. The most recent statistics show that more than 17,800 UK students took part in Erasmus (proportionately lower than in other EU countries), although non-EU countries such as Norway, Switzerland and Turkey also do so, which suggests that a Leave vote would not necessarily end UK participation.

So with an 'Out' vote the UK Government would save money through not having to provide student loans or maintenance to EU students, but equally the UK would lose access to EU research funding and possibly some reciprocal arrangements such as Erasmus. Universities, for example, are concerned about losing research funding; Dame Julia Goodfellow, president of Universities UK and vice-chancellor of the University of Kent, has said: 'British students benefit from being taught by the best minds from across Europe. Membership of the European Union is good for our universities and good for the science and research that improves people's lives.'

The UK is one of the largest recipients of research funding in the EU. Under the current 'Horizon 2020' research round, the UK secured 15.4 per cent of the available funds, more than every other Member State except Germany. Figures suggest that nearly 1,000 projects at 78 UK universities and research centres depend on funds from the European Research Council (ERC); indeed, the UK has more ERC-funded projects than any other country. All that could end in 2020 if the UK votes to leave the EU, while Brexit could also make life more difficult for the 15 per cent of academics working at UK institutions who are non-UK EU citizens. Advocates of an 'Out' vote, however, argue that universities could become more innovative once freed from EU regulations such as those governing clinical trials, while emphasising that however much research funding the UK receives it remains an overall net contributor to the EU budget.

In cultural terms, the EU also runs various programmes like the European Capital of Culture (won by Liverpool in 2008) and prizes for cinema and other creative industries. The European Union Prize for Contemporary Architecture, for example, carries a prize of €60,000 (with €20,000 for a special mention), something else that would be unlikely to survive following Brexit. Leaving the EU, however, would not mean the UK leaving the Eurovision Song Contest, for participant countries simply have to be members of the European Broadcasting Union, which is completely independent of the EU. Many non-EU countries such as Israel take part, while the UK started competing in 1957, 16 years before it joined the EEC.

Environment

When it comes to the environment, UK and EU law is strongly intertwined, the Single European Act providing that the EU 'preserve, protect and improve the quality of the environment;

to contribute towards protecting human health; and to ensure a prudent and rational utilisation of natural resources'.

Again, since the Maastricht Treaty was agreed in the early 1990s, EU directives have been adopted which aim to improve air quality, protect wildlife, clean up rivers and monitor standards of bathing water around the continent's beaches. Others have also imposed restrictions on landfill dumping, encouraged recycling, introduced lead-free petrol and improved animal welfare in food production.

The EU emissions trading scheme sets a decreasing cap for emissions from energy intensive sectors, and allocates or auctions emissions allowances, which can be traded on the open market. In other areas, for example wildlife protection and planning, the UK Government has expressed 'strong support' for the aims of the EU's environmental directives, so if the UK left the EU it would perhaps not lead to a big change in emphasis, although some fear that investment in 'green' jobs and growth could be threatened. Those who support Leave, however, argue that many EU directives relating to climate change and renewable energy targets cost the UK lots of money.

Scotland

Long before the creation of the European Union, Scotland had enjoyed a long history of intellectual, cultural, scientific and economic links with Europe. It formally became part of the 'Common Market' as part of the UK in 1973, and although it was more Eurosceptic than the rest of the country at the 1975 referendum, it is generally acknowledged that a higher proportion of Scots want to 'Remain' in the EU than their English counterparts.

This in turn has created a potentially complicated constitutional situation in which the majority of Scots could vote to 'Remain' part of the EU while a majority in England could vote to 'Leave', a referendum outcome the Scottish National Party – which wants to achieve 'independence in Europe' for Scotland – says would produce an 'unstoppable' momentum towards a re-run of the September 2014 referendum on Scottish independence.

But although the leader of the SNP and Scottish First Minister Nicola Sturgeon wants Scotland to become independent, she has been quite clear that she does not wish that to happen 'because the UK chooses to leave the European Union'. Rather she has promised to lead 'a positive and upbeat campaign to keep Scotland in the EU', citing benefits membership brings in terms of 'jobs, investment, social and employment protections and collective security'. 'It's not a perfect institution,' added Ms Sturgeon, 'and while I believe it would be best for Scotland to be in the EU as an independent member state, I believe it is better for us in all circumstances to stay in.'

Like her counterparts in Wales and Northern Ireland, the First Minister opposed the 23 June referendum date but says that now it has been confirmed 'we will get on with the job of campaigning for an "in" vote'. Nicola Sturgeon has also warned the UK Government and Britain Stronger in Europe campaign to 'learn the lessons' of Scotland's independence referendum and 'not lapse into scaremongering and fear', although many commentators believe there is a tension or contradiction between the party's opposition to one Union (the UK) and support for another (the EU). The SNP, meanwhile, has formed its own independent 'In' Europe campaign which it says will make a 'positive, progressive and upbeat' case for retaining Scotland's place in Europe. Europe minister Humza Yousaf is campaign director of 'SNP In Europe' and the SNP's Westminster Europe spokesperson Stephen Gethins his deputy. The SNP-controlled Scottish Government will also officially campaign for Scotland to Remain part of the EU, although none of its members will share a platform with pro-European Conservatives like the Prime Minister.

Some Scottish Nationalists, however, disagree with their leader's stance and think an independent Scotland would be better off 'Out'. Jim Sillars, a former deputy leader of the SNP and architect of its 1988 'independence in Europe' policy, has warned supporters of Scottish independence that remaining in the EU could damage their cause. In a pamphlet published for the Scotleave.eu campaign, 'The Logical Case', Sillars wrote:

13

Yes voters must ask: if the SNP succeeds through the Scottish vote in keeping the UK in the European Union, what will be different for the independence movement? The EU will return to the status quo, the UK's bluff having been called with no change towards Scotland. For Scotland, that means back in the same trap: our fate in their hands, with their distaste for the breakup of a member state the ruling factor in their attitude to our independence.

The former SNP leader Gordon Wilson has also suggested that if the UK votes to Leave the EU, then Scotland (as a 'territory') could apply to join the European Economic Area, thereby safeguarding Scotland's trading interests 'while avoiding the need for a very risky immediate referendum on [Scottish] independence'. Indeed Alex Bell, a former head of policy for the Scottish Government, believes that if England votes to 'Leave' the EU and Scotland to 'Remain', then 'there may well be a moment of indignation and a spike in nationalist fervour, but the reality is that it will also signal the death of the Scottish independence dream'.

The Scottish Labour Party, meanwhile, is as united as the SNP when it comes to the European referendum, with Ian Murray, its only MP, and all its declared MSPs in favour of the UK remaining part of the EU. Mr Murray and Scottish Labour leader Kezia Dugdale have emphasised that they will make 'a distinctly Labour case' for Scotland's place in the EU. 'There is a strong socialist case for staying in the EU,' Ms Dugdale has said. 'Working in solidarity with the other nations of the EU secures vital rights for workers and greater opportunities for our young people... Labour is Scotland's internationalist party. We believe working in solidarity with other nations makes us stronger.'

The former Liberal Democrat leader and North-East Fife MP Lord (Menzies) Campbell is doing a series of town-hall events as the public face of the European Movement in Scotland, saying he will make 'an unashamedly positive case' for a referendum 'In' vote and that the peace, stability and prosperity created by EU membership ought to be 'cherished'. The leaders of the Scottish Green Party also support a vote to 'Remain' in the EU.

On the 'Leave' side, the former Scottish Conservative MSP Brian Monteith is acting as head of press for the UK-wide Leave.EU campaign, while former Scottish Labour MP and minister Nigel Griffiths is fronting the Scottish Labour Leave group. One of the most prominent proponents of a 'Leave' vote in Scotland is the UKIP MEP David Coburn, although party leader Nigel Farage has described the campaign north of the border as 'a bit embryonic'. 'But let's not forget this great myth that somehow Scotland's wonderfully in love with the European Union,' he added. 'There's been precious little debate on this issue in Scotland.' On that point, a study for NatCen Social Research conducted between July 2015 and January 2016 found that only 17 per cent of Scots wanted to Leave the EU but another 43 per cent wanted its powers 'reduced'. A fifth were happy to 'leave things as they are'.

Meanwhile, the 'Scotland Stronger in Europe' (SSiE) campaign (part of Britain Stronger in Europe) has estimated that 336,000 Scottish jobs are linked to Scotland's trade with the EU, and Scottish exports like whisky worth £11.6 billion. It also highlights £750 million in structural funding between 2014 and

2020, more than £33 million from the Common Agricultural Policy over the next five years, as well as EU investment in Scottish broadband rollout (£10 million), environmentally-friendly buses in Aberdeen (£8 million), renewable energy projects in Orkney, Shetland and Caithness (£18 million) and the Falkirk Wheel (£1 million). In summary, it claims that while EU membership costs Scottish households less than a pound a day, it brings benefits worth £3,000 a year due to lower prices and greater jobs, trade and investment. John Edward, a former head of the European Parliament office in Scotland, is SSiE's chief campaign spokesman in Scotland.

If the UK does vote to 'Leave' the EU then it would produce a bit of a vacuum when it came to certain responsibilities. The Scotland Act of 1998 does not specify the powers of the Scottish Parliament, only those reserved to Westminster, so in the event of Brexit many European 'powers' would revert to Holyrood rather than Westminster, including policies relating to agriculture, fisheries, environment, justice, higher education and social policy. Just as the UK would have to decide whether or not to keep or amend previously European competences, so would the devolved Scottish Parliament.

Wales

Like Scotland, Wales is currently part of the European Union by virtue of being part of the United Kingdom. Areas such as West Wales and Valleys have generally received far more in EU structural funds (or economic aid) than other parts of the UK. Between 2014 and 2020, for example, it will receive a total of £1.8 billion for economic development and other important projects, while Welsh farmers share in payments from the Common Agricultural Policy.

Those who want Wales and the UK to 'Remain' part of the EU say this money would be lost in the event of an 'Out' vote, but those campaigning for Brexit say it is not 'European' funding but 'our' money, insisting that money would still be distributed to poorer areas of Wales if the UK leaves the EU, it would just come from the Welsh or UK Governments rather than Brussels. On a visit to Wales in February 2016, however, Prime Minister David Cameron said he could not 'guarantee' making up any shortfall in the event of an 'Out' vote, because 'we might be in quite difficult economic circumstances'.

Mr Cameron also told an audience at GE Aviation in Nantgarw that leaving the EU would put 100,000 jobs in Wales at risk, with the additional possibility of higher interest rates, unemployment and prices. But the chief executive of Leave. EU Liz Bilney said the real threat to Welsh jobs came from remaining part of an EU that had 'devastated the steel industry'. UKIP leader Nigel Farage also said the powers to protect the steel industry from the 'dumping' of cheap Chinese

14

imports had been 'given away' to Brussels, although the Prime Minister maintained that he and other European leaders had consistently backed anti-dumping tariffs.

In early March 2016 the ex-controller of BBC Wales, Geraint Talfan Davies, was named as chairman of 'Wales Stronger in Europe', a group campaigning for Wales (as part of the UK) to Remain in the EU. Like its parent body, Britain Stronger in Europe, this is a cross-party organisation and includes Plaid Cymru, the party which wants greater autonomy for Wales in the UK, perhaps even independence, its representatives including the former Plaid leader Lord (Dafydd) Wigley. Plaid MEP Jill Evans said that while there was 'a lot we would like to change about the EU' it could 'only do that from within'. 'The decision we make is about the kind of Wales we want to build', she added, 'and will affect generations to come.'

Conservatives in Wales, however, are split on Europe, with four of its 11 MPs (David Davies, James Davies, Chris Davies and the former Welsh Secretary David Jones) saying they want the UK to 'Leave' the EU, as does the leader of the Welsh Conservatives, Andrew R. T. Davies. All 25 Labour MPs, meanwhile, want to 'Remain' part of the EU, while UKIP in Wales wants to 'Leave' and the Liberal Democrats – as they are across the UK – are backing an 'In' vote on 23 June 2016.

Northern Ireland

As part of the United Kingdom, Northern Ireland has also been part of the European Union for the past 43 years. That period began with the height of The Troubles, a period of sectarian violence between Nationalists who wanted Northern Ireland to become part of the Republic of Ireland and Unionists who wanted to preserve its constitutional links with Great Britain. But despite their clear political differences, the three MEPs representing Northern Ireland (on behalf of Sinn Fein, the Democratic Unionist Party and Ulster Unionist Party) have generally co-operated in the interests of all voters.

The EU perhaps enjoys a higher profile in Northern Ireland than other parts of the UK, particularly as a source of funding. 'Objective 1' status between 1989 and 1999 resulted in £1.7 billion of structural funds, while the peace process from the late 1990s was rewarded with three dedicated 'peace programmes'. Northern Irish institutions like the Assembly and Executive, meanwhile, have gradually become more engaged with the EU and EU policy issues, in common with the UK's other devolved parliaments and assemblies.

Visiting Northern Ireland in February 2016, Prime Minister David Cameron highlighted the Common Agricultural Policy, warning that Brexit would be 'very, very damaging for Britain's farmers and for farmers here in Northern Ireland'. He also suggested that border arrangements between it and the Republic of Ireland could become 'harder', even though the Common Travel Area is separate from the Schengen Area.

15

The Northern Ireland Secretary Theresa Villiers, however, supports Northern Ireland (as part of the UK) leaving the EU, something she has described as the 'safer option', arguing that it would enable the UK 'to take back control over our country and making our laws and controlling our borders'. The other Northern Irish parties' positions are as follows:

- **Democratic Unionist Party (DUP).** Deputy leader Nigel Dodds said the DUP was recommending 'that our interests are better shared as a country and region outside the EU because it will give us control of our borders, our money and it will give us control of our laws', but party leader and Northern Irish First Minister Arlene Fraser also said individual members of the party would be free to take opposing sides in the debate, echoing the approach of the Conservative Party.

- **Sinn Fein.** Although Sinn Fein has long been critical of aspects of the EU and opposed both the accession of Ireland in 1973 and continuing UK membership in 1975, South Belfast MLA Máirtín Ó Muilleoir said all of Ireland had 'benefitted enormously' from membership: 'The EU has been a great supporter of our peace process and it's good in terms of the economy, there's really no argument at all. It's of much greater benefit to our businesses and agricultural community that we stay in the EU.'

- **Social Democratic and Labour Party (SDLP).** The former SDLP leader John Hume long championed the EU as an enabler of inward investment in Northern

Ireland, and indeed Claire Hanna, the current MLA for South Belfast, has said the benefits to Northern Ireland of EU membership were 'enormous in terms of financial support but also in terms of the value and the good of co-operation on this island and across the continent'.

- **The Alliance.** Alliance MLA Stewart Dickson points out that not only has Northern Ireland received structural and cohesion funds 'in excess of what we put in', but its businesses have benefited 'from trade barriers being brought down across Europe'. He added: 'While Alliance is unashamedly a pro-European party and will campaign to remain in, we are also not blind to the reforms needed. With too much power held at the Council and Commission, the EU Parliament needs to be strengthened.'

- **Ulster Unionist Party (UUP).** Following a special meeting of the party's executive committee on 5 March 2016 the UUP said it believed that 'on balance' Northern Ireland was better to 'Remain' in the EU, 'with the UK Government pressing for further reform and a return to the founding principle of free trade, not greater political union'. Like the DUP, the party says individual members are free to support both sides.

- **Traditional Unionist Voice (TUV).** TUV leader Jim Allister has described the Prime Minister's renegotiation as 'pitiful'. 'Not a single important aspect of our relationship with the EU will change as

15

a result of Mr Cameron's deal,' he said. 'Roll on the referendum in which TUV will campaign vigorously, and unitedly, and with others to extricate our nation from the EU. We have nothing to lose but our chains.'

- The **Greens** in Northern Ireland want the UK to stay in the EU, **UKIP** want to 'Leave,' and **NI21** wants to 'Remain' in a reformed Europe.

There have been suggestions that Brexit might disrupt the Northern Irish peace process, with some arguing that the province would 'descend back into violence' if the UK left the EU. Making a different point, Sinn Fein's Declan Kearney said Brexit would 'reinforce partition' and see the re-introduction of trading tariffs and customs posts, although the DUP have rejected such arguments as 'scare stories'. First Minister and DUP leader Arlene Foster said she wanted to see a campaign that was 'positively run', and also said the timing of the referendum – just weeks after elections to the Northern Ireland Assembly – was 'deeply regrettable but we must accept it and move on'. Meanwhile the Northern Ireland Stronger in Europe campaign, or 'NI-IN', forms part of the UK-wide Britain Stronger in Europe group.

Irish citizens in the UK

There is a centuries-long history of movement between Great Britain (England, Scotland and Wales) and Ireland, which continued after 1922 when Ireland was divided in two: the Irish Free State (later the Republic of Ireland, or simply 'Ireland') and Northern Ireland (which remained part of the UK). Census data from 2011 and several other statistical surveys suggest that around 500,000 people born in Ireland currently reside in the UK (although the total figure is in decline), while in 2006 around 291,000 British citizens lived in Ireland. At present, their respective rights are governed by two sets of arrangements: those provided by 'freedom of movement' under mutual membership of the European Union, and also British-Irish agreements that predate both countries' accession to the EU in 1973.

Between 1922, when the Irish Free State seceded from the United Kingdom (of Great Britain and Ireland), and the British Nationality Act of 1948, citizens of the Free State ('Eire' in British usage after 1937) continued to be recognised by the UK as British citizens, because technically Ireland constituted a British 'Dominion' (like Canada, Australia or New Zealand) within the wider British 'Commonwealth' (formerly Empire).

On 18 April 1949, however, Ireland chose formally to leave the Commonwealth – becoming a Republic rather than a Dominion – although the British Nationality Act made special provision for certain Irish citizens to retain the status of

16

'British subject' despite no longer being citizens of a Commonwealth country. Section 2 of the Act allowed 'citizens of Eire' who were British subjects before 1949 to apply at any time to remain so, provided they possessed a British passport, had worked for the Crown or had connections to other British territories. Anyone born in Ireland after 1948 could not claim the same right, although Irish citizens resident in the UK were entitled to apply for registration as a 'British citizen' (rather than subject) after one year's residence (later increased to five years).

The Ireland Act of 1949, meanwhile, recognised the end of Ireland's status as a British Dominion and also corrected an omission in the British Nationality Act, making it clear that regardless of the position under Irish law, those domiciled in Northern Ireland as of 6 December 1949 would not be deprived of British citizenship. It also confirmed that 'citizens of the Republic of Ireland' would not be treated as 'aliens' in the UK but rather on a par with those from Commonwealth countries (despite Ireland no longer forming part of the Commonwealth). The British Nationality Act of 1981 later confirmed this arrangement while requiring Irish citizens to apply for naturalisation as British citizens (rather than registration) after five years' residence in the UK.

In addition, British 'subjects' born in Ireland qualify for 'right of abode' in the UK. Their passports are marked 'European Union' (unlike other British subject passports) as their holders are also EU citizens. Since 1983 anyone born to a parent 'settled' in the UK has been automatically considered British, and Irish citizens are automatically deemed to be 'settled', a more favourable status than that granted to citizens of other

EU and European Economic Area Member States. This special status derives from the Immigration Act of 1971, which forms the legislative basis for the Common Travel Area (or CTA, comprising the UK, Ireland, Isle of Man and Channel Islands). The CTA means that Irish citizens arriving in the UK are not normally subject to any form of immigration control.

If the UK votes to 'Remain' in the EU then this double-layered UK and EU citizenship seems highly likely to remain unaltered, while if the UK votes to 'Leave', then the rights of Irish citizens in the UK are equally highly likely to be undisturbed, simply reverting to their pre-1973 form, which was largely unchanged by both countries' accession to the EU.

16

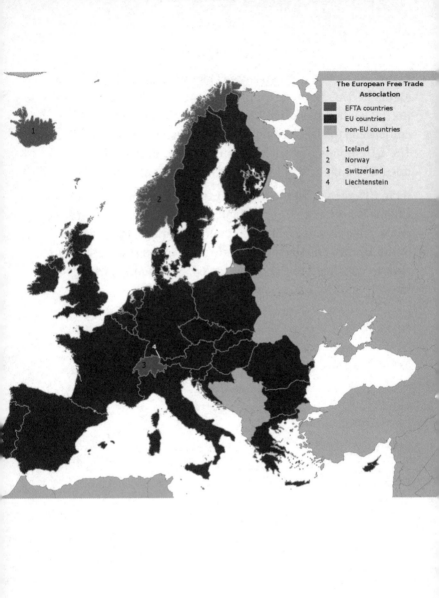

The European Free Trade Association

EFTA countries
EU countries
non-EU countries

1   Iceland
2   Norway
3   Switzerland
4   Liechtenstein

What Happens
if the UK Votes to Leave?

Formal procedures for a Member State to leave the EU were introduced as part of the 2009 Lisbon Treaty. Under its provisions, a country wishing to exit the EU must indicate as much, leading to negotiations over a withdrawal agreement between the Member State and the remainder of the EU. It would officially leave the EU on the date the withdrawal agreement came into effect, or two years after the date of notification if no agreement is reached, although it could take longer if both sides agreed to an extension. The Lisbon Treaty itself stresses that the 'process is unprecedented'.

Although withdrawal from the EU is unchartered territory, there are precedents from its previous incarnations. In 1962, for example, Algeria left the old 'Common Market' after becoming independent from France, while in 1985 Greenland (a Danish overseas territory) left the European Economic Community (EEC) following a 1982 referendum in which 52 per cent voted to leave. Those who want the UK to 'Leave' the EU generally emphasise its essentially political (and therefore flexible) nature; in other words, if voters back Brexit they believe the EU will be compelled to deal with the consequences as quickly and painlessly as possible.

But importantly, in negotiating Brexit, the EU would act *without* the involvement of the departing Member State, in

17

this case the UK. As a result, the UK would have a weak negotiating position and many commentators believe the EU would drive a hard bargain in order to discourage other Member States from considering withdrawal. The Prime Minister has been quite clear that if 'the British people vote to leave, there is only one way to bring that about, namely to trigger Article 50 of the treaties and begin the process of exit, and the British people would rightly expect that to start straight away'. During the negotiation period the UK would continue to abide by EU treaties and laws, but not take part in any decision making.

In the event of Brexit, meanwhile, the European Communities Act of 1972 would be repealed and the UK Government would have to review existing (and then draft new) laws covering farming, fishing, competition policy, regional aid and environ-mental standards in order to avoid a regulatory vacuum. It would also have to forge a new relationship with the rest of the EU, not least to deal with 2 million UK citizens with accrued rights resident in EU Member States and also its engagement with the Single Market's 'four freedoms', the free movement of goods, capital, services, and people. Crucially, if the UK wants to retain access to this post-Brexit, then it would also have to accept three things: continued budget contributions, continued free movement of labour and continued supremacy of EU law in terms of the Single Market, which of course are matters many want to escape by leaving the EU in the first place.

A detailed report from the London School of Economics identified the main options for the UK if it votes to 'Leave' the EU, each of which has strengths and weaknesses:

- The so-called 'Norwegian model', under which the UK would join the European Economic Area (EEA), which comprises Norway, Iceland and Liechtenstein, in order to retain access to the Single Market. Membership of the EEA, however, would require implementing EU rules governing the Single Market, much as the UK does at the moment, only without formal influence as a Member State. On the other hand, EEA members are not obliged to sign up to the single currency, Common Agricultural Policy, EU customs or the EU's foreign, security, justice and home affairs policies. A fee is necessary, and in 2011 Norway's contribution to the EU budget was £106 per capita, only 17 per cent lower than the UK's, so joining the EEA would not result in significant savings. It is what might be called a 'third way' between full EU membership and complete economic independence, although it would involve a loss of sovereignty. As a Norwegian politician once observed: 'If you want to run Europe, you must be in Europe. If you want to be run by Europe, feel free to join Norway.'

17

- The 'Swiss model', under which the UK would, like Switzerland, negotiate a series of bilateral treaties governing its relations with the EU and the Single Market, so separate agreements would cover issues like air traffic, fraud and pensions. Switzerland, meanwhile, is not a member of the EEA but is part of the European Free Trade Association (EFTA), which allows it to trade freely with the EU (apart from agricultural goods). As with Norway and the EEA,

Switzerland has little influence over how the EU programmes in which it participates actually work, and again like Norway it makes a financial contribution to cover costs, which in recent years has averaged around £53 per capita. Again, the Swiss model would involve a loss of sovereignty, although it is not subject to the European Court of Justice and the EU's social and employment regulations.

- Re-joining EFTA. When the UK opted out of joining the original European Economic Community in 1957 it founded EFTA as an alternative, and could revisit this option in the event of Brexit. Doing so would guarantee UK goods tariff-free access to the EU and also make sure the UK did not impose tariffs on goods imported from the EU, but it would not provide for free movement of people or trade in services between the two. The UK, however, would not be in the Single Market and costs could rise as a result, while it – like other non-EU countries – would probably have to consider the Norwegian or Swiss models in conjunction with membership of EFTA.

- The UK could also join the EU's customs union, like Turkey, accepting the EU's external tariffs but without having a say on how they were set. As a result, the UK would not face tariffs on its exports to the EU although it would have to sign up to all the relevant EU rules. It would have access to goods markets, meanwhile, but not those for services.

- The World Trade Organisation (WTO) option. If the UK chose not to join the EEA, EFTA or negotiate a series of bilateral treaties, its trade with the EU (and indeed the rest of the world) would be governed by the WTO, which has 161 members. But this would mean the UK's exports would be subject to tariffs, raising costs for British firms and reduced access to the Single Market. Free movement between the UK and EU would also cease, although capital flows would probably continue. On the other hand, the UK would be free to set its own tariffs on imports, it would make no contribution to the EU budget, and political sovereignty would be greater than the other options outlined above, with potentially lower regulation and no oversight from the European Court of Justice.

- Looking beyond Europe. Outside the EU, the UK would represent itself in international trade negotiations and could opt to seek closer integration with countries beyond Europe, for example the 'BRIC' nations, North America or fellow members of the Commonwealth. One option might be joining Canada, Mexico and the United States as a member of the North American Free Trade Agreement (NAFTA), but the UK might find itself with less trading clout than it has within the EU, particularly if trading deals like the Transatlantic Trade and Investment Partnership (TTIP) conclude successfully, while the UK would no longer enjoy the benefits of around 60 Free Trade Agreements the EU has negotiated with other countries. The farther countries are from one another, meanwhile, the less trade there tends to be, and of course the UK is closer to the EU than it is to

17

North America, although it could get round this by creative tailoring of policy.

The remaining EU Member States, of course, would have to endorse whatever relationship the UK settled upon with the Single Market. Asking that question, researchers from the University of Edinburgh and the German think tank d|part, surveyed more than 8,000 people in six EU countries – Germany, France, Ireland, Poland, Sweden and Spain – and found that nearly half the Germans surveyed were in favour of a post-Brexit UK staying within the Single Market, although only a quarter of French respondents agreed. People in Poland and Ireland were also sympathetic with 50 per cent and 41 per cent respectively backing continued trade with the UK, although most Swedes questioned were undecided. Sir John Major, the former Conservative Prime Minister, has warned that it 'is blithe optimism on a Panglossian scale for the "leave" campaign to assume that our partners – having been re-buffed and deserted in an EU diminished by our departure – will be well disposed and eager to accede to our demands'. Rather he believes 'the reverse will be true':

> Resentment will be deep. The broken relationship is more likely to be poisonous than harmonious. The UK will have chosen to leave and, by so doing, will have gravely weakened the whole of the EU. Our partners will not wish to reward us for that – indeed, they may well be more inclined to resist our demands to discourage other nations from leaving it... In time, the EU will no doubt do a trade deal with us – but it will certainly not be a sweetheart deal: and negotiating it is likely to be harder and harsher than the optimists believe.

In March 2016 the UK Government produced its own analysis of what would happen if the UK voted to Leave the EU:

- Outside the EU, the analysis suggests products made in the UK and exported to the EU would face higher tariffs, for example on sugar.

- Withdrawal from the EU is 'unprecedented' and thus highly unpredictable.

- Two million UK citizens live in other EU Member States and receive access to pensions, health care and other public services as a result. 'There would be no requirement under EU law for these rights to be maintained if the UK left the EU.'

- Brexit would have a 'profound impact' on the UK's economy because of tariffs on British exports like cars, while economic growth and the value of the pound could also be affected.

- There would also be a 'serious impact' on farmers as a result of losing subsidies from the Common Agricultural Policy and tariffs on agricultural imports.

- If the UK votes to Leave' then it could weaken EU-wide action such as sanctions against North Korea and action targeting terrorist groups.

- Customs checks might be created between Northern Ireland and the Republic of Ireland with possible restrictions on movement between the two. The British Overseas Territory of Gibraltar may also lose the right for its citizens to move freely in and trade with Spain.

17

Many of these points have been contested by campaigners supporting a 'Leave' vote. They argue that the UK Government is deliberately exaggerating the consequences of Brexit, and that so big is the UK's trading clout that the EU would be foolish not to agree to a mutually beneficial deal. UKIP leader Nigel Farage, however, says he does not want the UK to be part of the Single Market in the event of an 'Out' vote, nor have even the status of Norway or Iceland, and therefore any post-Brexit arrangement would become much harder to obtain.

If the UK votes to 'Leave' the EU it could also have an impact on several aspects of the domestic political scene:

- **The Prime Minister might have to resign, although David Cameron has formally denied this possibility. His Conservative Party, however, would be badly split over Brexit, and many senior figures would most likely call for him to go. Such an outcome could also impact on the most likely successor, with Boris Johnson's chances (having supported an 'Out' vote) improving relative to those of Chancellor George Osborne (who is backing 'In').**

- **In Scotland the SNP might also demand a second independence referendum, particularly if a majority of Scots have voted to 'Remain' in the EU while a majority in England have supported 'Leave'. The Scottish Government, however, will probably only do so if support for independence reaches around 60 per cent as a result of Brexit, which is not guaranteed.**

- **Northern Ireland's Deputy First Minister Martin McGuinness has also said he would demand a 'border poll' in the event of the 'political and economic**

17

game-changer' caused by a 'Leave' vote, not least the creation of a 'hard' border between northern and southern Ireland. He said it would be a 'legitimate test of political opinion that would threaten no-one'. The Republic of Ireland, meanwhile, is clearly concerned about what Brexit would mean for its status in the EU, given its close links with the UK.

- Finally, there is a theoretical possibility that MPs could reverse a vote to 'Leave' given that referendums in the UK are not legally binding. A withdrawal agreement would have to be ratified by Parliament and, according to the House of Commons Library, even if MPs voted against, 'the treaty can still be ratified if the Government lays a statement explaining why the treaty should nonetheless be ratified and the House of Commons does not resolve against ratification a second time within 21 days (this process can be repeated ad infinitum)'. In another hypothetical scenario, two thirds of MPs could initiate an early general election and campaign on a promise to keep the UK in the EU, despite the outcome of the referendum. That would produce two competing mandates and very likely provoke extremely bitter political disagreement, not only in Parliament but among voters across the UK.

Sir John Major has also argued that a UK Brexit would mean that 'the political influence of the EU would be diminished – especially when considered against the power of the United States or China'. 'Without the UK,' he adds, 'Europe – the cradle of modern civilisation – would fall to a lower significance.'

What Happens
if the UK Votes to Remain?

If voters support the UK remaining in the European Union by a majority then the Prime Minister's renegotiation agreement – agreed in Brussels in February 2016 – will begin to take effect, including changes to child benefit, an 'emergency brake' on EU migrants' in-work benefits, an opt-out from 'ever-closer union' and protection for the City of London. Beyond that, a vote to Remain in the EU is a vote to maintain the status quo – with certain caveats.

Some Eurosceptics, meanwhile, have speculated as to what might happen should the UK vote to 'Remain' in the EU. The Conservative MEP Daniel Hannan, for example, has said: 'If we vote to remain in, we shall be voting to be part of everything that is coming: the integration of our tax systems, defence policies, welfare rules and, yes, immigration policies. Brussels, not Westminster, will decide how many asylum seekers come here. We cannot say we haven't been warned.' This ignored, however, the existence of a UK 'veto' covering some of those areas.

Pro-Europeans have also ruminated on the relationship between the UK and the EU should Brexit be rejected. The European political commentator Kirsty Hughes, for example, has argued that even if all four parts of the UK – England, Scotland, Wales and Northern Ireland – vote to 'Remain' in

18

the EU, the implementation of David Cameron's deal (along with the referendum experience) could 'reinforce the UK's current semi-detached, low influence role in the EU'.

There is one other 'Remain' scenario, in which the UK as a whole has voted to stay in the EU but a majority of voters in England have voted to 'Leave'. Some Eurosceptics in the Conservative Party and UKIP might argue that the result is illegitimate, placing pressure on the internal constitutional politics of the United Kingdom, particularly the Union between Scotland and England. 'UKIP and other Eurosceptics', writes Kirsty Hughes, 'may suddenly find themselves strong converts to a dissolution of the UK, and even unlikely proponents of an independent Scotland.'

Another point is that the UK's relationship with the EU – and indeed the EU itself – has rarely been static, usually being subject to reform every few years. The same is true of the 27 other Member States, and it seems likely that if the UK votes to 'Remain' then the process of reform, however imperfect, will continue. Some have spoken, for example, of a 'two-tier' or 'twin-speed' European Union in which the 19 members of the single currency, or Eurozone proceed on a different basis (and pace) than non-Euro Member States like the UK.

Other commentators, mainly those who want the UK to 'Leave' the EU, have predicted that the Union will decline and might even break up under the pressure of the crisis in the Eurozone (from which Greece or another southern European country might eventually exit) and the migrant crisis, which has already led to border closures within the Schengen Area. They argue that while the EU served a purpose in the wake of

18

the Second World War, it no longer adequately reflects the world in the early 21st century.

Finally, despite having voted to 'Remain' within the EU, the question of the UK's membership might also be revisited in a future referendum, although most likely only after a reasonable period of time has elapsed since that being held on 23 June 2016.'

18

Who Supports Remain and Leave?

Leave/Out

Members of the UK Cabinet who want the UK to Leave the EU:

Iain Duncan Smith, Work and Pensions Secretary
Chris Grayling, Leader of the House of Commons
John Whittingdale, Secretary of State for Culture
Theresa Villiers, Secretary of State for Northern Ireland
Michael Gove, Secretary of State for Justice
Priti Patel, Minister of State for Employment*
Boris Johnson, Mayor of London**
Zac Goldsmith, Conservative candidate for Mayor of London
(May 2016)***

* Members who attend Cabinet

** Attends Conservative political cabinet meetings

*** Does not attend Cabinet

At the time of publication, 130 Conservative MPs wanted the UK to 'Leave' the EU, as did seven from Labour, eight from the DUP and one from UKIP.

19

> There are many positive aspects to leaving the EU. We will make our own laws again in our own parliament. We will rediscover the skills of blue-water diplomacy and rise to the challenge of global markets. It could be the spark we need to re-energise our nation: a

challenge and an opportunity. To remain in the EU is in my judgement a more dangerous option for British security in its deepest sense – economic, political, military and social – than remaining in a dysfunctional EU dragged down by a failing Eurozone. Remaining in the EU is risking more than leaving.

Lord (David) Owen, former SDP leader and Foreign Secretary

I am positive about leaving the EU because I believe rather than saying it is a leap in the dark, I think it is a stride into the light. It is about hope versus pessimism and people will vote for that... [the UK] has stood alone in war but it has also defined trade around the world... Britain is a phenomenal country. It has stood alone and fought for freedom. It has been a global trader, it can again be a global trader.

Iain Duncan Smith MP, Work and Pensions Secretary

The EU has become a sprawling, petty, inefficient, self-obsessed bureaucracy with a vociferous appetite for controlling nearly every aspect of our lives, however tiny. It is wonderful that we have had over 70 years of peace in most of Europe, but that has not been brought about by Eurocrats issuing directives stipulating the maximum suction power of a vacuum cleaner... It is true that leaving the EU would involve some uncertainties and even a few risks. But virtually every substantial human achievement involves having the guts to go it alone. How Britain would look outside

19

of the EU will be up to us. Staying doesn't mean no change.

Mark Littlewood, Institute of Economic Affairs

If Britain remains chained to Brussels after this charade [the Prime Minister's renegotiation] we'll be in a weaker position than before. We'll be the country that made Eurosceptic noises for decades but capitulated when it mattered. The EU's bureaucracy, courts and politicos will see us as all-bark, no-bite moaning minnies.

Tim Montgomerie, political commentator

If you cannot make your own laws, if you cannot control your own borders, you are not an independent, sovereign nation and I want to live in an independent sovereign nation... Let me tell you, as a former defence secretary, our security does not lie in the European Union. The cornerstone of our security is Nato. It is Nato that has kept the peace in Europe since World War 2.

Dr Liam Fox MP, former Conservative Defence Secretary

We would repeal the 1972 European Communities Act, which establishes the primacy of EU law over our own UK law. The morass of EU regulation, much of which is costly, unnecessary and undesirable, would become UK regulation, which we would then be free to accept, repeal or amend as our national interest requires. And

19

we would continue to trade with the EU, as the rest of the world does today, almost certainly assisted by a bilateral free trade agreement, which they need far more than we do. Above all, we would become once again a self-governing democracy, with a genuinely global rather than a little European perspective. We would prosper, we would be free, and we would stand tall. That is what this referendum is all about.

Lord (Nigel) Lawson, former Chancellor of the Exchequer

Voting to stay in means remaining on a conveyor-belt whose far end we can't see. The Schengen and euro crises are deteriorating – which is one reason that the government was in a rush to hold the referendum at the earliest possible date. Staying in means more risk and more cost. It's safer to take back control.

Daniel Hannan MEP, South East England (Conservative Party)

[The EU is] built on neo-liberal economic principles which are iron-clad and unchangeable... I'd rather take my chance with changing things in Britain than waiting for change in Bulgaria or in Poland or in Germany. The people of Greece were crushed underfoot by this neo-liberal consensus on which the EU and its main institutions are built... I don't want us to suffer the same fate as them.

George Galloway, former Labour and Respect MP

19

I think unless there are some extremely significant changes we should get out... you cannot be dictated to by thousands of faceless civil servants who make these rules and you say, "Oh, wait a minute, is that right?" Then they argue about [finances] but we buy more from them than we sell to them... I feel certain we should come out.

Sir Michael Caine, actor

The Democratic Unionist Party has always been Eurosceptic in its outlook. At every stage in this European negotiation process we had hoped to see a fundamental change to our relationship with Europe. In our view we see nothing in this deal that changes our outlook. Therefore we will on balance recommend a vote to leave the EU.

Arlene Foster MLA, leader of the DUP and First Minister of Northern Ireland

Almost nothing the EU has proposed or enacted has benefited Britain – our trawler fleet has been devastated by the Common Fisheries Policy while our taxpayers have found themselves massively subsidising inefficient French and Polish farmers under the Common Agricultural Policy... This newspaper has always been hostile to the dilution of national sovereignty that EU membership entailed, but it has also always acknowledged that economic arguments were key... As a heavy net importer from the EU we are simply too important a market for the

19

EU nations to risk cutting ties with... Our political class bought into the European experiment after losing confidence in our nation and accepting the inevitability of decline. They viewed Europe as a life raft and clambered on board. The British people never took that view. Now it is Europe that is in decline and Britain that is being held back. It is time to break free.

Editorial, *Daily Express*

It's my view that, after 30 years of writing about this, we have a chance actually to do something, I have a chance actually to do something and I would like to see a new relationship based more on trade, on co-operation but as I say with much less of this supra-national element... after a great deal of heartache I don't think there is anything else I can do, I will be advocating Vote Leave, or whatever the team is called – I understand there are many of them – I think that is basically, because I want a better deal for the people of this country, to save them money, and to take back control.

Boris Johnson MP, Mayor of London

I actually believe the EU is holding this country back... we cannot control our borders, limit the number of people who come here, do trade deals. I do not believe we can take decisions in the national interest when we are part of the European Union... By leaving we would bring more jobs, more business, more trade in the United Kingdom – that is the prize we get for leaving the European Union... if we are outside the European Union

19

we can take better decisions – things that will benefit this country in a way that right now we simply cannot.

Chris Grayling MP, Leader of the House of Commons

Our membership of the European Union prevents us being able to change huge swathes of law and stops us being able to choose who makes critical decisions which affect all our lives. Laws which govern citizens in this country are decided by politicians from other nations who we never elected and can't throw out. We can take out our anger on elected representatives in Westminster but whoever is in Government in London cannot remove or reduce VAT, cannot support a steel plant through troubled times, cannot build the houses we need where they're needed and cannot deport all the individuals who shouldn't be in this country. I believe that needs to change. And I believe that both the lessons of our past and the shape of the future make the case for change compelling.

Michael Gove MP, Secretary of State for Justice

[I was asked] if, after leaving office, Lady Thatcher had come to the view that Britain should leave the European Union. I said yes (I think it happened after the Maastricht Treaty in 1992), although advisers had persuaded her that she should not say this is public since it would have allowed her opponents to drive her to the fringes of public life.

Charles Moore, journalist and biographer of Margaret Thatcher

19

Remain/In

Members of the UK Cabinet who want to Remain in the EU:

David Cameron, Prime Minister
George Osborne, Chancellor of the Exchequer
Philip Hammond, Foreign Secretary
Theresa May, Home Secretary
Sajid Javid, Business Secretary
Stephen Crabb, Secretary of State for Wales
Justine Greening, International Development Secretary
Jeremy Hunt, Health Secretary
Greg Clark, Communities and Local Government Secretary
Patrick McLoughlin, Transport Secretary
Elizabeth Truss, Environment Secretary
Oliver Letwin, Chancellor of the Duchy of Lancaster
Nicky Morgan, Secretary of State for Education
David Mundell, Secretary of State for Scotland
Baroness Stowell of Beeston, Leader of the House of Lords
Michael Fallon, Secretary of State for Defence
Amber Rudd, Secretary of State for Energy
Matt Hancock, Paymaster General*
Greg Hands, Chief Secretary to the Treasury*
Mark Harper, Chief Whip*
Anna Soubry, Minister for Small Business*
Robert Halfon, Minister without Portfolio*
Jeremy Wright, Attorney General*

* Members who attend Cabinet

At the time of publication, 162 Conservative MPs wanted the UK to 'Remain' in the EU, as did 215 from Labour, 54 from the SNP, eight from the Liberal Democrats, four from Sinn Fein, three from the SDLP, three from Plaid Cymru and one from the Greens.

> The businesses we lead represent every sector and region of the UK. Together we employ hundreds of thousands of people across the country. Following the prime minister's renegotiation, we believe that Britain is better off staying in a reformed European Union. He has secured a commitment from the EU to reduce the burden of regulation, deepen the Single Market and to sign off crucial international trade deals.
>
> Business needs unrestricted access to the European market of 500 million people in order to continue to grow, invest and create jobs. We believe that leaving the EU would deter investment, threaten jobs and put the economy at risk. Britain will be stronger, safer and better off remaining a member of the EU.

Letter to *The Times* signed by around 200 business leaders including the chairmen or chief executives of 36 companies from the FTSE 100

> Europe is going to emerge stronger than ever, provided it stays united and builds common responses to these challenges. Now obviously, the United States has a profound interest in your success, as we do in a very strong United Kingdom staying in a strong EU.

John Kerry, US Secretary of State

> I would like to see the pro-European side to get out there with a bit of passion and vigour and

19

determination, and stand up for what we believe... not just as a matter of economic realism but as a matter of political idealism... What frustrates me is that Britain has got a great opportunity to lead in Europe... person for person it is in the Premier League of systems. Our destiny as a country is to lead in Europe and we can and we should. And once this is out of the way, with some strong leadership in our own country we will.

Tony Blair, former Labour Prime Minister

Londoners' interests clearly lie with Britain remaining in Europe. It is not in London's interest to turn our back on the trading area on which so many of our jobs depend. And it's not in our interest to walk away from the co-operation that helps us tackle crime and terrorism. Walking away from Europe would be both irresponsible and dangerous.

Sadiq Khan MP, Labour candidate for Mayor of London

For [football] clubs, free movement plays a big role in transfers and players' contracts. Players from the EU can sign for UK clubs without needing a visa or special work permit, making it quicker and easier to secure top talent from across Europe to come and play in our leagues. Indeed, there are nearly 200 Premier League footballers alone who have benefited from this arrangement. Leaving the EU could have a big impact on foreign players, as independent analysis has shown that two-thirds of European stars in England would not meet automatic non-EU visa criteria and therefore

19

might be forced to leave. Losing this unhindered access to European talent would put British clubs at a disadvantage compared to continental sides.

Lady (Karren) Brady, vice-chairman of West Ham United

I feel European even though I live in Great Britain, and in Scotland. So of course I'm going to vote to stay in Europe. Oh my God, it would be madness not to. It would be a crazy idea not to. We should be taking down borders, not putting them up.

Emma Thompson, actress

In the Second World War, my father fought against the Germans. In the First World War, my grandfather fought, my great-grandfather fought 20 years before that... Having a European Union – there are so many benefits and I just hope sense will prevail when it comes to having the vote on it.

Sir Richard Branson, businessman and founder of the Virgin Group

Forty-four percent of what this country exports goes to the EU... the EU's the biggest game in town. Let's not poke that big customer in the eye.

Richard Reed, co-founder of Innocent Drinks

19

I believe that we are stronger, better off and safer inside Europe than we would be out on our own. To claim that the patriotic course for Britain is to retreat, withdraw and become inward looking is to misunderstand who we are as a nation. I will not allow anyone to tell me I'm any less British because I believe in the strongest possible Britain for business, for our security and our society.

Lord (Stuart) Rose, former Executive Chairman, Marks & Spencer

I'm a supporter of the EU but when I vote for Britain to remain in the EU in June, I will not be voting for the status quo – let me be clear about that. I will not be voting for the EU which has sought to impose eye-watering austerity, at the expense of the ordinary citizen not the rich, but on Ireland, Greece, Spain, Portugal and elsewhere. I will not be voting for the EU which is seeking to stitch-up a pro-big business trade deal – TTIP – behind the backs of the people of Europe. Above all, I will not be voting for David Cameron's renegotiation package – a deal designed to protect the financial interests in the City of London which control the Conservative party and to pander to anti-migrant and anti-welfare sentiment.

Len McCluskey, General Secretary, Unite

In the referendum campaign Labour will be making it clear we stand up for public ownership and accountability. Our party is committed to keeping Britain in the EU because we believe it is the best framework for European trade and cooperation and is in the best interests of the British people. But we also want to see progressive reform in Europe: democratisation, stronger workers' rights, sustainable growth and jobs at the heart of economic policy, and an end to the pressure to privatise and deregulate public services.

Jeremy Corbyn MP, Leader of the Labour Party

The Rock has protected key trade routes and British interests for centuries. Being British and trading is what Gibraltar has long thrived on. We are part of the great British family who will be voting on June 23. Gibraltar will be voting to stay in the EU. It is just too important not to. There is nothing romantic about this. Gibraltar's economy, despite the nagging directives and Eurocracy, has thrived since we became part of the EEC in 1973. Our finance centre is as well regulated as the City's and our gaming industry is a world leader and model for compliance. If Britain leaves the EU, who knows what will happen to these precious advantages we enjoy?

Fabian Picardo, Chief Minister of Gibraltar

While the [Prime Minister's] renegotiation was successful. It wasn't central. It's not central in the minds of most people. People across Scotland, across all of Britain, will make up their mind on much bigger issues. Given that Europe is the world's biggest market, will we be more prosperous if we remain or leave? Given that this is a dangerous and uncertain world, are we safer and more secure by staying

19

alongside our closest friends and neighbours? Or turning our backs on them? Given the scale of international challenges of a global economy, climate change and the refugee crisis – are we better to face these together or alone? ... If you want a Britain that is prosperous, secure, a Britain that matters, then you are voting to keep Britain in Europe.

Tim Farron MP, Leader of the Liberal Democrats

Ultimately many of the crises we face, from climate change, to the plight of refugees and a rotten financial system, don't respect national borders and isolationism offers no solution. By working with our neighbours we have a chance to rise to the challenges of the 21st century. It's this vision of a better Europe that's also bringing together refugees, environmentalists, academics, students and politicians tonight to launch a different campaign: Another Europe is Possible. We want the UK to stay in Europe but we also want radical change. Our demands are varied, and the reforms we want will take time. But our core belief, that we're better off working together, is resolute. The time has come to take back the EU referendum debate from the men in grey suits.

Caroline Lucas MP, former Green Party leader

The Church recognises that the decision taken will impact our country and communities for generations to come and we call for a positive debate on the European Union that takes account of its role in promoting peace, security and international cooperation. While each individual will reflect and come to their own decision with integrity, the Church of Scotland takes the position that in this time of enormous international challenge, it is better for us as a country to remain within the EU.

Rt Rev Dr Angus Morrison, Moderator of the General Assembly of the Church of Scotland

It's riskier to leave the European Union than to stay in it because change is always riskier. However, risk should not be automatically considered a bad thing. If you are risk averse you should probably vote to stay in the EU. If, however, you are of the view that you want change you should vote out. Honestly, I'm risk averse. At the moment I am probably 55/45 for staying in Europe. However, I, like everybody else, am still doing my research on this issue and what it means for me and my country.

Martin Lewis, Money Saving Expert

How much you pay for your holiday really does depend on how much influence Britain has in Europe. As a result of Britain's membership, the cost of flights has plummeted while the range of destinations has soared. That's why EasyJet believes the benefits far outweigh the frustrations and why the UK is better off as part of the EU.

Carolyn McCall, Chief Executive, EasyJet

19

This best of both worlds, out of the single currency, out of the Schengen borders agreement, out of the ever-closer union but in the things that work for Britain, that give us jobs, that give us security, that give us the ability to make sure we have a stronger and safer world, I think that is something worth fighting for.

David Cameron MP, Prime Minister

The EU is a coming together of independent states that choose to pool some of their sovereignty to better tackle those issues that don't respect national boundaries – like climate change, energy security and the refugee crisis. It's not a perfect institution – and while I believe it would be best for Scotland to be in the EU as an independent member state, I believe it is better for us in all circumstances to stay in.

Nicola Sturgeon MSP, SNP leader and First Minister of Scotland

What people want to hear is how to build a European future which acts on the environment, which faces down the multi-nationals, which shows solidarity when faced with a refugee crisis, which acts together against austerity, which respects its component nations, which co-operates on great projects like a super grid across the North Sea and which revitalises the concept of a social Europe for all of our citizens. That is a Europe worth voting for.

Alex Salmond MP, SNP MP for Gordon and former First Minister of Scotland

19

The EU is far from perfect, and no one should be in any doubt that this deal must be part of an ongoing process of change and reform – crucial if it is to succeed in a changing world. But in my view – for reasons of security, protection against crime and terrorism, trade with Europe, and access to markets around the world – it is in the national interest to remain a member of the European Union.

Theresa May MP, Home Secretary

Fundamentally, this referendum was always going to be about far bigger issues than those David Cameron has been negotiating on. It will be about the future we want for our children and the kind of country we want to be. It will be about the three million or more jobs that are linked to our trade with Europe. It will be about the investment and growth that being part of the biggest market in the world brings us, bigger than China, bigger than the USA. It will be about protections for workers and consumers, our ability to confront terrorism, crime, climate change and Putin's Russia. And about keeping our borders secure – inside Europe, but outside the Schengen borderless zone. Leaving would put all of that at risk and diminish Britain's global influence. Of course the EU needs to be reformed. But the fundamentals are still as clear as they ever were: Britain needs to be leading, not leaving. Building on the EU's achievements, not throwing them away. A vote to Remain is the only way to ensure future

19

generations enjoy the benefits of Europe, as
consumers or workers.

Alan Johnson MP, former Labour Home Secretary

It's about the money in people's pockets. The £3,000
per household, right across Wales. On jobs there are
200,000 people who depend on our membership of the
EU up and down Wales. Airbus... Tata Steel... I am not
prepared to put that at risk... I don't want Wales and
Britain to surrender our place in the world. A strong
confident country shaping the future of Europe in an
uncertain world.

Carwyn Jones AM, First Minister of Wales

We believe the United Kingdom is stronger as a result
of its membership. And we believe the EU is stronger
with the UK's involvement. That's our view.

Joe Biden, Vice-President of the United States

The United States values a strong UK in a strong
European Union, which makes critical contributions to
peace, prosperity, and security in Europe and around
the world.

Barack Obama, President of the United States

Whether I'm sitting in a railway concourse in Brussels
or pottering down the canals of southwestern France
or hurtling along a motorway in Croatia, I feel way
more at home than I do when I'm trying to get

something to eat in Dallas or Sacramento. I love Europe, and to me that's important... isn't it better to stay in and try to make the damn thing work properly? To create a United States of Europe that functions as well as the United States of America? With one army and one currency and one unifying set of values? Britain, on its own, has little influence on the world stage. I think we are all agreed on that. But Europe, if it were well run and had cohesive, well thought-out policies, would be a tremendous force for good.

Jeremy Clarkson, presenter of *Top Gear*

In the referendum campaign Labour will be making it clear we stand up for public ownership and accountability. Our party is committed to keeping Britain in the EU because we believe it is the best framework for European trade and cooperation and is in the best interests of the British people. But we also want to see progressive reform in Europe: democratisation, stronger workers' rights, sustainable growth and jobs at the heart of economic policy, and an end to the pressure to privatise and deregulate public services.

Jeremy Corbyn MP, Leader of the Labour Party

19

The Rock has protected key trade routes and British interests for centuries. Being British and trading is what Gibraltar has long thrived on. We are part of the great British family who will be voting on 23 June. Gibraltar will be voting to stay in the EU. It is just too important not to. There is nothing romantic about this. Gibraltar's economy, despite the nagging directives and Eurocracy, has thrived since we became part of the EEC in 1973. Our finance centre is as well regulated as the City's and our gaming industry is a world leader and model for compliance. If Britain leaves the EU, who knows what will happen to these precious advantages we enjoy?

Fabian Picardo, Chief Minister of Gibraltar

While the [Prime Minister's] renegotiation was successful, it wasn't central. It's not central in the minds of most people. People across Scotland, across all of Britain, will make up their mind on much bigger issues. Given that Europe is the world's biggest market, will we be more prosperous if we remain or leave? Given that this is a dangerous and uncertain world, are we safer and more secure by staying alongside our closest friends and neighbours? Or turning our backs on them? Given the scale of international challenges of a global economy, climate change and the refugee crisis – are we better to face these together or alone? [...] If you want a Britain that is prosperous, secure, a Britain that matters, then you are voting to keep Britain in Europe.

Tim Farron MP, Leader of the Liberal Democrats

Ultimately, many of the crises we face, from climate change to the plight of refugees and a rotten financial

19

system, don't respect national borders and isolationism offers no solution. By working with our neighbours we have a chance to rise to the challenges of the 21st century. It's this vision of a better Europe that's also bringing together refugees, environmentalists, academics, students and politicians tonight to launch a different campaign: Another Europe is Possible. We want the UK to stay in Europe but we also want radical change. Our demands are varied, and the reforms we want will take time. But our core belief, that we're better off working together, is resolute. The time has come to take back the EU referendum debate from the men in grey suits.

Caroline Lucas MP, former Green Party leader

Neutral

We need a new union that gives people's rights primacy over and above the interests of transnational capital, and that defends the free movement of migrants not just within Europe but also from outside it. Whatever the outcome of the coming UK referendum, War on Want will continue to join with others from across the continent (and beyond) in the project to develop this new European reality from below.

John Hilary, Executive Director, War on Want

As for Britain's role in Europe, that should be a matter for the British people to decide and for your American partners to respect whatever decision you make. Our

19

alliance, our partnership and our affection for your nation will continue regardless of the road you choose.

Marco Rubio, Republican candidate for US President

My hope and prayer is that we have a really visionary debate about what our country looks like. From those who want to leave; what would it look like? What would Britain look like, having left? What would be its attitude internationally? What would be its values? What are the points of excitement, of contributing to human flourishing? How does that liberate the best that is within us? And from those who want to stay, how would we change the European Union? How would we make it more effective if we remained in it? What's our vision?

Justin Welby, Archbishop of Canterbury

The Queen remains politically neutral, as she has for 63 years. We would never comment on spurious, anonymously sourced claims. The referendum will be a matter for the British people.

A Buckingham Palace spokesman following claims in the *Sun* newspaper that the monarch had told former Deputy Prime Minister Nick Clegg that the EU was 'heading in the wrong direction'.

19

Frequently Asked Questions

What is the European Referendum?
The UK has been a member of the European Union since 1973. The Conservatives promised to have a referendum – or vote – on either staying in the EU or leaving in their 2015 election manifesto. They won that election, so the referendum is going to take place.

What is the European Union?
The European Union is an economic and political partnership comprising 28 European countries. It has its own parliament and other common institutions, while 19 of its 'Member States' use a single currency known as the Euro.

What renegotiated terms of membership have been agreed?
An 'emergency brake' on migrants' in-work benefits, restrictions on child benefit for the children of EU migrants living overseas, an opt-out from 'ever-closer union' and safeguards against 'discrimination' for the UK not being part of the Eurozone.

When is the referendum?
In February 2016 the Prime Minister, David Cameron, announced that the referendum would take place on Thursday, 23 June 2016.

What will the referendum question be?
'Should the United Kingdom remain a member of the European Union or leave the European Union?' So voters will

20

either put a cross next to 'Remain' or 'Leave', also known as the 'In' or 'Out' options.

Who wants to Remain or stay 'In' the EU?

There is only one group campaigning for the UK to stay part of the EU, called 'Britain Stronger in Europe', while there are also groups called 'Scotland Stronger in Europe', 'Wales Stronger in Europe' and 'Northern Ireland Stronger in Europe – NI-IN'.

Who wants to Leave or come 'Out' of the EU?

There are two main groups campaigning for the UK to leave the EU, 'Vote Leave' and 'Grassroots Out'. By 15 April 2016 the Electoral Commission will designate one of those the 'lead' campaigner.

Who will be able to vote in the referendum?

British, Irish and Commonwealth citizens over the age of 18 who are resident in the UK, as well as UK nationals who have lived overseas for less than 15 years. Citizens of EU countries, except for Ireland, Malta and Cyprus, however, will not be allowed to vote, while members of the House of Lords and Commonwealth citizens in Gibraltar will.

When do the referendum campaigns begin?

The official campaign period will be between 15 April and 23 June, although campaigning essentially began as soon as the Prime Minister announced the date of the referendum.

What are the rules for campaigning?

The Electoral Commission will oversee this, but the two official campaigns will get access to a grant of up to £600,000,

20

an overall spending limit of £7 million, campaign broadcasts and free mailshots.

How much can political parties spend?

Over and above the two official campaigns, this is determined by how many votes each party got in the 2015 general election, so the Conservatives can spend the most at £7 million, Labour £5.5 million, UKIP £4 million and the Liberal Democrats £3 million. The SNP, Greens, Plaid Cymru and other parties that got fewer than 5 per cent of the vote will be limited to £700,000 each.

What are the main arguments to 'Leave' the EU?

Those opposed to EU membership say the money saved could be reinvested in public services, while they also want to regain control over the UK's borders and migration policies.

What are the main arguments to Remain in the EU?

Those in favour of EU membership say the Single Market benefits every British household by around £3,000 each year, while they believe the UK has more influence in the modern world as part of the EU.

What does 'Brexit' mean?

The term is a commonly-used abbreviation for 'Britain' and 'Exit' from the EU.

What do businesses think?

Larger businesses tend to favour EU membership while smaller businesses are more likely to back withdrawal. There are, of course, exceptions in each case.

Will there be referendum TV debates?

Yes, the BBC is planning three debates, one on 19 May from Glasgow (aimed at younger voters), a *Question Time* special on 15 June and on 21 June a much bigger debate at Wembley Arena. It is not yet clear if the Prime Minister will take part.

What is the expected result of the referendum?

Most recent opinion polls show voters in the UK are roughly evenly divided between leaving and staying in the EU, although in Scotland there is a stronger balance towards 'Remain'. At the time of going to press the number of 'don't knows' was running at between 17 and 20 per cent, meaning the referendum vote could go either way.

20

UK/EU Timeline

1946   Winston Churchill calls for a 'kind of United States of Europe' during a speech at Zurich University, although he does not necessarily envisage it including the UK.

1948   The European Union of Federalists organises a Congress at The Hague in 1948 with a view to drawing up a European constitution. But the United Kingdom rejects a federal approach and later an inter-governmental 'Council of Europe' is created, which in turn produces a European Convention on Human Rights.

1949   The Washington Treaty is signed by the United States, Canada and ten Western European states including the UK, thus forming the North Atlantic Treaty Organisation (NATO). This operates on the principle that if one member state is attacked then all the others will come to its defence.

1950   French Foreign Minister Robert Schuman delivers the 'Schuman Declaration', a plan for France and Germany – and any other state that wished to join – to pool coal and steel production. He argues that solidarity in production would make war between France and Germany 'not merely unthinkable but materially impossible'.

1951 The Treaty of Paris is signed by 'the Six' (Belgium, France, Germany, Italy, Luxembourg and the Netherlands), establishing a European Coal and Steel Community (ECSC) governed by a 'High Authority' and a 'Common Assembly'. The Dutch and Germans insist on a 'Council of Ministers' comprising representatives from other Member States as a counterbalance to the supra-national High Authority. Over time this trio of bodies evolve into the European Commission, European Parliament and Council of Ministers.

1952 Jean Monnet becomes the first president of the High Authority and the ECSC guarantees German coal to the French steel industry while providing funds to upgrade Belgian and Italian coal mines. Germany, meanwhile, begins dismantling its steel cartels in order to gain international respectability.

1954 In response to the Korean War the US insists that Europe must contribute more to its own defence and that Germany must rearm. In 1952 the six ECSC members agree to create a 'European Defence Community' in which German soldiers would join a 'European Army'. But the French parliament delays ratification and ultimately rejects the proposal in 1954; the UK also considers joining, but ultimately does not.

1955 Foreign ministers from the six ECSC Member States meet in Messina, Italy, and agree to re-launch the European integration project, leading to the 'Spaak Report' and, later, the Treaty of Rome.

1957 'The Six' sign the Treaty of Rome to establish the 'European Economic Community' (EEC) and, via a separate treaty, the European Atomic Energy Community (Euratom). The aim of the EEC is to create a 'Common Market' and customs union as well as ensuring free movement of capital and labour (France also negotiates subsidies for its farmers). Euratom's goal is the joint development of nuclear energy.

1958 The EEC starts work and quickly establishes itself as the most important of the various European institutions, with its Commission, Council of Ministers and advisory Parliamentary Assembly (appointed rather than elected), whose first session is held in Strasbourg. A European Court of Justice is also created to interpret the Treaty of Rome and officiate in disputes regarding EEC decisions.

1959 The Organisation for European Economic Co-operation (OEEC), comprising Austria, Denmark, Norway, Portugal, Sweden, Switzerland and the UK, decide to establish a European Free Trade Association (EFTA). The UK was one of the leading founding members of EFTA.

1960 The EFTA is launched, aiming (like the EEC) to establish free trade but opposing uniform external tariffs and supra-national institutions.

1961 The UK government led by Conservative Harold Macmillan applies for membership of the EEC, as does Denmark.

1962   The Parliamentary Assembly changes its name to the European Parliament.

1963   French president Charles de Gaulle says he doubts the political commitment of the UK to European integration and vetoes its (and Denmark's) application for membership. Reports suggest he has worries about English taking over as Europe's main language, the UK's close relationship with the US, and his vision of an amplified French voice in world affairs.

1965   A Treaty to merge the executives of the three Communities – ECSC, EEC and Euratom – is signed in Brussels.

1967   The above Treaty comes into force creating the 'European Community' with a single Council and Commission for three previous 'Communities'. The UK, meanwhile, applies to join for the second time, and once again de Gaulle says 'non!'

1968   The European Community's customs union is completed.

1972   Norway holds a referendum on membership of the Community, but a majority votes against.

1973   The UK, Ireland and Denmark all join the Community, the last two following successful referendums.

1974   British Foreign Secretary James Callaghan makes a statement calling for major changes to the Common Agricultural Policy (CAP), 'fairer methods of financing the Community budget' and solutions to monetary problems. Later that year the Community's members decide to hold meetings three times a year as the 'European Council', agree direct elections to the European Parliament, resolve to set up a 'European Regional Development Fund' and work towards economic and monetary union.

1975   The UK government, led by Labour's Prime Minister Harold Wilson, puts re-negotiated terms of membership to a June referendum. Members of his Cabinet campaign both for and against, but two thirds of voters support continuing membership.

1978   The European Council establishes the 'European Monetary System' based on a European Currency Unit (called the ECU) and an Exchange Rate Mechanism (ERM). From the following year the ECU is used in travellers' cheques and bank deposits, and all the Community's members join the ERM – except the UK.

1979   The first direct elections to the European Parliament take place in June. The UK is divided into large first-past-the-post regions and sends 81 Members (MEPs) to sit in Strasbourg and Brussels, the majority of whom are Conservative.

1981   Greece becomes the tenth member of the European Community.

1984   A draft Treaty on the establishment of the 'European Union' is passed by the European Parliament, while the European Council in Fontainebleau agrees on a budget 'rebate' for the UK following heavy lobbying by the Conservative Prime Minister Margaret Thatcher. Conservatives once again win (UK) elections to the European Parliament.

1985 Commission president Jacques Delors proposes that by the end of 1992 the Community ought to remove a series of barriers to free trade and the free movement of capital and labour in order to create a 'Single Market', reviving the goal of European integration in the process. The UK's Commissioner Lord Cockfield was instrumental in conceiving of the Single Market in a white paper published that year.

1986 Following the transition to democracy in both countries, Spain and Portugal join the Community and the Single European Act is signed. The European flag is also adopted by Community institutions and flown for the first time outside the Commission's Berlaymont HQ in Brussels.

1987 The Single European Act comes into force, creating 'an area without frontiers in which the free movement of goods and persons, services and capital is ensured'. Turkey applies to join the Community.

1988 The European regional aid budget is doubled as a quid pro quo for poorer southern Mmember States who complain that market liberalisation benefits the more developed northern countries.

1989 The third UK elections to the European Parliament produces a Labour majority for the first time.

1990 The European Council in Rome launches two inter-governmental conferences, one on Economic and Monetary Union (EMU) and the other on Political Union. The UK finally joins the ERM.

1991 The Maastricht Treaty is signed, paving the way for monetary union as well as a 'Chapter' on social policy. The UK negotiates an opt-out from both. The Treaty also creates a 'European citizenship' giving Europeans the right to live, work and vote in elections anywhere in the Community.

1992 Maastricht means the European Community now has three 'pillars', the European Community (EC), the Common Foreign and Security Policy (CFSP) and Justice and Home Affairs (JHA). Meanwhile the UK is forced out of the ERM, intended to harmonise EU member states' financial systems before the creation of a single currency called the Euro.

1993 The Treaty on the European Union (rather than European Community) comes into effect, while the Maastricht Treaty has a rough ride in national referendums. Denmark accepts it in a second ballot having secured a UK-like opt-out on monetary union and several other areas, while in France it is narrowly endorsed by voters. In the UK Conservative Prime Minister John Major survives a back-bench rebellion over accepting the Treaty.

1994 At UK elections to the European Parliament – now with 87 UK MEPs – Labour once again wins the most seats.

1995 Austria, Finland and Sweden join the European Union, bringing membership to 15. The Schengen Agreement also comes into force between Belgium, France, Germany, Luxembourg, the Netherlands, Portugal and Spain, with an undertaking to lift border controls. The UK and Ireland stay out of the agreement, instead forming a Common Travel Area (CTA) within the British Isles. Norway once again rejects membership in a referendum.

1997 The Amsterdam Treaty is signed, emphasising citizenship, the rights of individuals and giving more powers to the European Parliament. Laws on employment and discrimination are also strengthened, while the 'Social Chapter' of the Maastricht Treaty becomes an official part of EU Law. The Schengen Agreement also became part of EU law, with opt-outs for the UK and Ireland. The UK also secured an opt-out from future AFSJ (Area of Freedom, Security and Justice) legislation, as did Ireland.

1998 The European Central Bank is established in Frankfurt to oversee the Euro, while accession (membership) negotiations begin with Cyprus, the Czech Republic, Estonia, Hungary, Poland and Slovenia. Soon talks also begin with Romania, Slovakia, Latvia, Lithuania, Bulgaria and Malta.

1999 The entire European Commission led by Jacques Santer resigns when the Committee of Independent Experts publishes a report highlighting allegations of fraud, mismanagement and nepotism. In the UK there are tensions over France's ban on British beef during the 'mad cow' disease outbreak. Elections to the European Parliament return slightly more Conservative than Labour MEPs, while the relatively new United Kingdom Independence Party (UKIP) wins three seats under a new proportionate electoral system.

2000 Denmark votes against joining the single currency in a referendum, while the Charter of Fundamental Rights of the European Union is formally declared.

2001 The Treaty of Nice is signed, reforming the institutional structure of the European Union to allow for eastward expansion. Ireland, however, rejects the Treaty in a referendum.

2002 On 1 January Euro notes and coins enter circulation in 12 participating Mmember Sstates, Austria, Belgium, Finland, France, Germany, Greece, Ireland, Italy, Luxembourg, the Netherlands, Portugal and Spain. The UK, meanwhile, announces 'five tests' which have to be passed if it is also to join, although public opinion is against. In another referendum, Ireland accepts the Treaty of Nice.

2003 A convention headed by former French President Valery Giscard d'Estaing spends more than a year drafting the EU's first constitution, its goal being to simplify existing Treaties to make them more easily understood by European citizens. But at an inter-governmental conference heads of state and government fail to agree a final text.

2004 Elections to the European Parliament in June include ten new Member States, Cyprus, the Czech Republic, Estonia, Hungary, Latvia, Lithuania, Malta, Poland, the Slovak Republic, and Slovenia, and therefore a reduced tally of 78 UK MEPs (UKIP increases its representation to 12 seats). A 'Constitution for Europe' is finally signed.

2005 Voters in France and the Netherlands reject the new Constitution in referendums, plunging its future into doubt.

2006 Negotiations on Turkey's accession to the European Union are suspended after it refuses to open its sea and air ports to ships and planes from Cyprus, with which it has a long-standing territorial dispute.

2007 Bulgaria and Romania join the EU, bringing membership to 27, although there is doubt as to whether they are ready. The Lisbon Treaty (which essentially took the place of the failed European Constitution by simplifying and merging existing treaties) hands greater powers to the Union's institutions in Brussels, but UK Prime Minister Gordon Brown misses the televised ceremony at which it is signed. The UK's AFSJ opt-out is preserved, to which is added the option of exercising a 'block opt-out' from all AFSJ measures in 2013.

2008 Ireland rejects the Lisbon Treaty in a referendum.

2009 In June 736 MEPs are elected to represent 500 million Europeans in 25 Member States, while the

UK elects 72 representatives, including 13 from UKIP.
Ireland accepts the Lisbon Treaty in a second
referendum.

2011	David Cameron clashes with Brussels over plans to
introduce a levy on banks and restrict London's
financial sector. He pledges to win back powers for
the UK.

2013	In a speech at Bloomberg in London David Cameron
pledges to hold a referendum after renegotiating the
UK's relationship with the EU. At the end of the year,
the UK Government exercises its right to opt-out of
all AFSJ legislation currently in force but
simultaneously applies to re-join the most
significant measures, including the European Arrest
Warrant.

2014	In elections to the European Parliament, UKIP wins
24 MEPs, more than any other UK party. The UK
government passes legislation facilitating a
referendum on the EU by the end of 2017.

2015	The Conservatives win an overall majority in a UK
general election (UKIP win just one seat), meaning a
referendum will take place in the next two years.

2016	The remaining provisions of the European
Referendum Act come into force and European
Council president Donald Tusk publishes a draft
agreement on the UK's membership of the EU,
followed by a summit with the other member states
in February. The referendum follows in June.

2018 If the UK votes to Leave the EU, it is required to complete its departure within two years of invoking Article 50 of the Lisbon Treaty, which means it would cease to be a Member State in the summer of 2018.

Further Reading

Books

David Baker & Pauline Schnapper (2015), *Britain and the Crisis of the European Union* (AIAA)

Roger Bootle (2015), *The Trouble with Europe: Why the EU isn't Working, How it Can be Reformed, What Could Take its Place – New and Updated Brexit edition* (Nicholas Brealey)

David Charter (2012), *Au Revoir, Europe: What if Britain left the EU?* (Biteback)

David Charter (2016), *Europe In or Out: Everything You Need to Know* (Biteback)

David Conway (2014), *With Friends Like These...: Why Britain Should Leave the EU – and How* (Civitas)

Hugo Dixon (2014), *The In/Out Question* (CreateSpace)

Daniel Hannan (2016), *Why Vote Leave* (Head Zeus)

Roger Liddle (2014), *The Europe Dilemma: Britain and the Drama of EU Integration* (I. B. Tauris)

John McCormick (2013), *Why Europe Matters: The Case for the European Union* (Palgrave Macmillan)

Denis MacShane (2015), *Brexit: How Britain will Leave Europe* (I. B. Tauris)

David Owen (2015), *The UK's in-Out Referendum: EU Foreign and Defence Policy Reform* (Haus)

Hugo Young (1999), *This Blessed Plot: Britain and Europe from Churchill to Blair* (Macmillan)

Online

https://www.gov.uk/guidance/review-of-the-balance-of-competences

https://fullfact.org/europe/

http://infacts.org/

http://ukandeu.ac.uk/

http://businessforbritain.org/change-or-go/

Glossary

Common Agricultural Policy (CAP)

The EU's system of subsidies for farmers.

Common Travel Area (CTA)

A passport-free travel area comprising the UK, Ireland, Isle of Man, Guernsey and Jersey.

Council of the European Union (or Council of Ministers)

Where ministers from Member States meet and take legislative decisions.

Economic and Monetary Union (EMU)

The mechanism underpinning the single currency, or Euro.

Euro

The EU's single currency, currently used by 19 Member States.

European Central Bank (ECB)

Controls monetary policy for the 'Eurozone'. Based in Frankfurt.

European Commission

Executive body of the EU.

European Commissioner

Member of the European Commission cabinet, one representing each Member State.

European Council

An EU institution where heads of state and government from Member States meet to decide policy and strategy.

European Court of Human Rights (ECHR)

A court in Strasbourg that upholds the European Convention on Human Rights. Not part of the EU.

European Court of Justice (ECJ)

This is part of the EU and is based in Luxembourg. It upholds and interprets EU law, with one judge from each Member State.

European Economic Area (EEA)

The EU plus Norway, Iceland and Liechtenstein. This takes part in the Single Market and, as a result, adopts all relevant EU laws.

European Economic Community (EEC)

Predecessor of the EU.

European External Action Service (EEAS)

The EU's foreign ministry and diplomatic service.

European Free Trade Association (EFTA)

Comprises Norway, Iceland, Liechtenstein and Switzerland, originally set up in 1960 as an alternative to the EEC.

European Parliament

The EU's directly-elected legislative body comprising 751 members (MEPs) including 73 from the UK.

European Union (EU)
An alliance of 28 Member States.

Four freedoms
The free movement of capital, goods, people and services, the basis of the Single Market.

Member State
A country which is a member of the EU.

Qualified Majority Voting (QMV)
The means by which the Council of the EU reaches decisions; it gives greater weight to smaller countries via a complex formula.

Schengen Area
A visa-free travel zone comprising 26 countries and named after a border town in Luxembourg.

Single Market
The EU's customs-free internal trading block established by the Single European Act of 1986.

Structural funds
EU aid for certain projects in poorer or developing areas of Member States.

Subsidiarity
A principle enshrined in the Maastricht Treaty that the EU shall only act if its objectives cannot be implemented at the lowest possible level of government in its Member States.

Appendices

UK European Parliament election results

Date	Members	Result
7 June 1979	81	60 Conservative, 17 Labour, 1 SNP, 1 DUP, 1 UUP, 1 SDLP
14 June 1984	81	45 Conservative, 32 Labour, 1 SNP, 1 DUP, 1 UUP, 1 SDLP
15 June 1989	81	45 Labour, 32 Conservative, 1 SNP, 1 DUP, 1 UUP, 1 SDLP
9 June 1994	87	62 Labour, 18 Conservative, 2 Liberal Democrat, 2 SNP, 1 DUP, 1 UUP, 1 SDLP
10 June 1999	87	36 Conservative, 29 Labour, 10 Liberal Democrat, 3 UKIP, 2 Green, 2 SNP, 2 Plaid Cymru, 1 DUP, 1 UUP, 1 SDLP
10 June 2004	78	27 Conservative, 19 Labour, 12 UKIP, 12 Liberal Democrat, 2 Green, 2 SNP, 1 Plaid Cymru, 1 DUP, 1 UUP, 1 Sinn Féin
4 June 2009	72	25 Conservative, 13 UKIP, 13 Labour, 11 Liberal Democrat, 2 Green, 2 BNP, 2 SNP, 1 Plaid Cymru, 1 DUP, 1 Sinn Féin, 1 UCU-NF

| 22 May 2014 | 73 | 24 UKIP, 20 Labour, 19 Conservative, 3 Green, 2 SNP, 1 Liberal Democrat, 1 Plaid Cymru, 1 DUP, 1 Sinn Féin, 1 UUP |

UK EU Commissioners

Between 1973 and 2004 the United Kingdom had two European Commissioners, and a single Commissioner from 2004 until present:

Christopher Soames (1973–77)
Lord (George) Thomson of Monifieth (1973–77)
Lord (Christopher) Tugendhat (1977–85)
Roy Jenkins (1977–1981, as President of the Commission)
Ivor Richard (1981–85)
Lord (Arthur) Cockfield (1985–89)
Stanley Clinton Davis (1985–89)
Bruce Millan (1989–95)
Leon Brittan (1989–99)
Neil Kinnock (1995–2004)
Chris Patten (1999–2004)
Lord (Peter) Mandelson (2004–08)
Lady (Catherine) Ashton (2008–14)
Lord (Jonathan) Hill (2014 –)

Member States of the European Union (with year of entry)

Austria (1995)	Belgium (1958)
Bulgaria (2007)	Croatia (2013)
Cyprus (2004)	Czech Republic (2004)
Denmark (1973)	Estonia (2004)
Finland (1995)	France (1958)

Germany (1958)	Greece (1981)
Hungary (2004)	Ireland (1973)
Italy (1958)	Latvia (2004)
Lithuania (2004)	Luxembourg (1958)
Malta (2004)	Netherlands (1958)
Poland (2004)	Portugal (1986)
Romania (2007)	Slovakia (2004)
Slovenia (2004)	Spain (1986)
Sweden (1995)	United Kingdom (1973)

Candidates for Membership of the European Union

Albania

Montenegro

Serbia

The former Yugoslav Republic of Macedonia

Turkey

(Switzerland made an application for membership of the EU in 1992, but later suspended it, while in 2009 Iceland also applied and formal negotiations began the following year, although this was suspended in 2013 and withdrawn in 2015.)

Potential Candidates for Membership of the European Union

Bosnia and Herzegovina   Kosovo

Luath Press Limited

committed to publishing well written books worth reading

LUATH PRESS takes its name from Robert Burns, whose little collie Luath (*Gael.*, swift or nimble) tripped up Jean Armour at a wedding and gave him the chance to speak to the woman who was to be his wife and the abiding love of his life.

Burns called one of 'The Twa Dogs' Luath after Cuchullin's hunting dog in Ossian's *Fingal*. Luath Press was established in 1981 in the heart of Burns country, and now resides a few steps up the road from Burns' first lodgings on Edinburgh's Royal Mile.

Luath offers you distinctive writing with a hint of unexpected pleasures.

Most bookshops in the UK, the US, Canada, Australia, New Zealand and parts of Europe either carry our books in stock or can order them for you. To order direct from us, please send a £sterling cheque, postal order, international money order or your credit card details (number, address of cardholder and expiry date) to us at the address below. Please add post and packing as follows: UK – £1.00 per delivery address; overseas surface mail – £2.50 per delivery address; overseas airmail – £3.50 for the first book to each delivery address, plus £1.00 for each additional book by airmail to the same address. If your order is a gift, we will happily enclose your card or message at no extra charge.

Luath Press Limited
543/2 Castlehill
The Royal Mile
Edinburgh EH1 2ND
Scotland

Telephone: 0131 225 4326 (24 hours)
email: sales@luath.co.uk
Website: www.luath.co.uk